Extending Narrative Therapy

A collection of
practice-based papers

collected by

Dulwich Centre Publications

ADELAIDE
SOUTH AUSTRALIA

Copyright © 1999 *by* Dulwich Centre Publications
ISBN 0 9586678 9 6

published by
Dulwich Centre Publications
Hutt St PO Box 7192
Adelaide, South Australia 5000
phone (61-8) 8223 3966 fax (61-8) 8232 4441

printed & manufactured in Australia by:
Graphic Print Group, Richmond, South Australia

100% recycled
paper

cover artwork by: Danni McLean, Pt Adelaide, South Australia
typeset, layout & design by: Jane Hales, Melrose Pk, South Australia

Contents

iii

Contents (cont'd)

Introduction

Welcome to this collection of easy-to-read, engaging practice-based papers all of which received great feedback when they were first published.

A quick glance through the contents page shows the diversity of ways in which therapists, students, teachers, parents, young people and community workers are extending upon what has come to be known as 'narrative therapy and community work'.

For many of the authors, this is the first book their writings have appeared in and this has made the process of gathering these papers together particularly delightful. Seeing the ways in which people are developing their own creative ways of working continually offers us a sense of renewal. We hope this is also true for you as readers.

The papers in this collection range from descriptions of new possibilities for externalising conversations; to experiences of group work; to examples of community work influenced by narrative ideas. Other sections include 'In our own voice' in which authors write of the ways they have re-authored aspects of their own experience, 'Talking about sexual abuse', 'Reflections on practice', and 'New ways of introducing narrative therapy'.

Our hope in putting together this collection is that it will interest practitioners who wish to keep in touch with the ways in which people are extending upon narrative ideas in their own contexts. The papers included describe work occurring in schools, on gatherings, in sexual assault services, in family homes, therapy rooms and teaching contexts.

We hope the diversity and creativity within these pages encourages you to extend upon your own work and also ... to write about it!

David Denborough
Staff Writer
Dulwich Centre Publications

Cheryl White
Editor
Dulwich Centre Publications

PART I

Extending
Externalising
Conversations

1

Talking with Dak [1]

('dak' is a colloquial term for marihuana) [2]

by

Kathy Cronin-Lampe

with

Puni Tufuga, Shannon TeKira & Amber Herbert [3]

Dedication:

This paper is dedicated to our friend Tennessey who played an important part in the groups described here, and who died on 2nd September 1997.

We feel it's really important to talk about Dak because in our lives it's always there. You are always having to make the choice whether to take Dak or leave it. You can get it real easy. If you know someone who knows someone you're sweet. In every suburb in Hamilton there's a seller, there's a dealer. Dak is everywhere. It's here in the school. As we're young, we believe we should be doing stuff like sports and not have to rely on drugs.

One of our best friends, Tennessey, died and I'm sure Dak had a lot to do with it. Once this happens to someone who you feel heaps of love for, it gives you a whole new perspective. When he was using he was getting more and more depressed even though he thought it was doing him good. Dak stopped him from talking to people and it made him lie to those he loved. He wanted to talk to someone but he felt he couldn't because then they'd find out about his addiction and he'd be so embarrassed.

Finally Tennessey took a stand against Dak. He joined our group. He came off it. He felt so proud. But then he got lured back in. All his mates smoked it. He was more isolated when he was off it, more alone. Hie mates were important to him. He wanted to be off it. He hated what it did to him and people who were important to him. But being off it was hard too. I don't think he wanted to tell anyone he'd got back into it. He'd have felt so shamed-out. Always one of his friends was still smoking it and saying 'we'll stop tomorrow', or 'after this joint ...' I reckon Dak has caused so much suicide.

Puni Tufuga

In mid 1997 a number of students in a variety of ways approached me (Kathy Cronin-Lampe) and Ron Cronin-Lampe in our roles as counsellors at Melville High School in Hamilton, New Zealand, to talk about Dak and its role in their lives and the lives of people they cared about. Some of these students were wanting help to 'kick Dak', while others were wanting to find out more about it and then decide on its usefulness.

Ron and I decided that we would ask all these students whether they would like to be a part of an experiment, whether they would be happy to form one large group to work together as third and fifth form students. We explained that we wanted to try out some new ways of talking about problems, and that we wanted to make a video which could be used as an educational and informative resource. Both groups expressed enthusiasm for this idea and seemed keen to share their work on video, especially when we said that we wanted to present it to our university colleagues as part of our studies.

When we gathered as a larger group for the first time we introduced the idea of having an externalising conversation directly with the problem - in this case with Dak. We talked with the group about the wealth of knowledge in the group about Dak, and asked them if they were interested in articulating all that they knew about it. We discussed what kinds of things they might ask Dak to find out about the influence that it was having among them. We discussed with the group our ideas about interviewing the problem to try and understand how 'it' works. The group was enthusiastic about being part of our project and felt that they would benefit from the exercise.

Interviewing Dak

Interestingly, the two members of the group who insisted on taking up the role of Dak were the two who had kicked it out of their lives. The rest of the group decided that they would like to write their own questions as investigators and they then shared their questions with one another. We wrote their questions on the board, and more questions were generated. These included:

- *What do you aim to do to people?*
- *What do people use you for?*
- *Who invented you? Are you the same all the time?*
- *What do you want for your users?*
- *What dreams do you have for the future?*
- *What influence do you want to have in the world?*
- *How did people first hear about you?*
- *How come they still want to know about you?*
- *Who persuades people to start with you?*
- *How do most people feel after their first experience of you?*
- *Why do people keep coming back to you?*
- *How do you get people 'hooked' on you?*
- *How are you affecting our community?*
- *What are some of the risks people take when they invite you into their lives?*
- *Do you invite people to be honest and open and share with your family/teachers and the Principal?*
- *How do you feel about principals/ guidance counsellors/the police?*

- *What makes you so powerful?*
- *Do you play tricks on people to make them think you're 'cool'?*
- *What is your interest in money?*
- *What do you give to people who can't afford you?*
- *How do you invest the money you earn?*

Here Puni and Shannon who played the role of Dak speak about their experience of the discussion:

Puni: *When I took on the role of Dak with Shannon I was angry. I was wanting to provoke the others so that they would stand up, fight back. I wanted them to get angry and to see what Dak is, what it does to people. I was giving them that information so they could stand up. When we were in the role of Dak we had to be really dominant, really strong in what we were saying. For every question we had to answer really fast because if we faltered they'd think of another question. We had to have the power because Dak has to have the power. I've seen it. That's what it does. It just takes power off people.*

At first me and Shannon were just bumming them out and they were getting quiet. When they asked us questions about how do we get them to smoke us and have us in their lives, we said, 'We have our sellers and we have our dealers and we try to get them to get to know you. We get them to give you a free smoke because then you'll like us. We'll get the friends that we've already got into our web to get you hooked. After that we don't care because we've done it. We don't care if you're hooked. As long as you're buying it then we're selling it.' It was great.

Shannon: *I thought we were really cool as Dak. When we were winning they looked real stink [stupid]. When Dak had the power I felt good.*

Amber, who was one of the students playing the role of investigative reporter explains what it was like to be on the receiving end of Dak's power:

It was like every question we asked they always had a straight out answer for it. It made us feel real weak - like it was taking us over.

After the group had asked Dak the questions that they wanted answers to, we stopped the video and discussed how they had felt as Dak had answered their questions. This brought about a heated discussion about how powerful and arrogant Dak was and how it had written them off as 'dicks'. We talked about the friends of Dak, and also about the times when Dak had failed to influence people in the ways that it had wanted and desired to.

Questioning Dak about rejection

The reporters decided that they would ask Dak some more questions in order to find out a 'counter-plot' to the story it was telling them. Again, we wrote the questions on the board and added to them as they requested.

- *What happens when people say 'NO' to you?*
- *What happens to your dreams when you get rejected?*
- *Dak, how have people managed to avoid you?*
- *How and when does a person's voice outmatch yours?*
- *How do you deal with resistance and determination?*
- *Does determination frustrate your plans for people?*
- *How come some people have managed to kick you?*
- *How come some people have never been interested in you?*
- *How come some of the people who know you reckon you 'suck'?*
- *How are you going to get back into the lives of people who have turned against you?*
- *What do fitness and good health say about you?*
- *What voice do you use on those who have rejected you?*
- *What do you say about those who won't try you, or who defy you?*
- *Some people control you, how does it feel that you don't control them?*
- *People we know have kicked you so that they could get fit, what do you think about this?*
- *How does the media reject you?*

- *If groups of people stand together against you, what will you do?*
- *Who is most likely to stand against you?*
- *What is it that people do to shun you? How do they do it?*
- *How do you know when to get lost?*

On reflection, Ron and I both felt that we did not give enough attention to this stage. In hindsight it probably would have been good to allow more time in between these sessions so that the above questions could have been developed more extensively, and so that a more thorough reflection on the impact and influence which Dak' insisted that it was having in the community could have taken place.

The two people who were in the role of being Dak reported to us that they were feeling strong, and that the questions being asked were easily swept aside. With this display of dominance by Dak, the group soon abandoned their investigation as reporters, and resumed asking questions about the problem and trying to argue with Dak. The group finished this part of the session and many expressed that they were feeling a bit deflated and overcome by the immensity of the problem. We discussed this as a group, talked about 'Where to from here?' and decided what we'd like to do next. Many in the group stated that this experience and project was indeed 'real' to them, and reflected their own positioning in relation to the problem at a personal level. Dak was having its way with some of them, but for the first time it seemed they weren't happy about this. They no longer wanted to feel silenced by Dak. They wanted to begin the next session with re-screening the video.

Re-engaging with Dak

At the beginning of the next session the group watched the video again, and Ron and I noticed a definite change in positioning. Many did not want to be reporters, they wanted to talk to Dak, to trip it up and catch it out. 'We want to bum Dak out' they stated, and they wanted to tell Dak about how it was affecting their lives and 'make it listen'. They wanted to gather together as a group and stand against it. Even though this was not strictly following our original hopes for the video, it was still very much following the spirit of Roth & Epston (1998) and seemed to be a continuation of a problem-externalising conversation.

As Amber describes:

When we watched the video again and saw what was happening I felt stupid that something like that can take over so easily. It made us annoyed. It was when we heard Dak saying that it could win so much, thinking that it could take power off us, that we finally realised what was going on. We clicked onto what Dak was doing to us. Although it was kind of a game it was serious too.

The group then began to question Dak again, using many of the questions listed above, and the reporters exhibited both persistence and determination when Dak became evasive. Again, Amber explains:

We started asking good questions, tough questions. In the end Dak didn't have so many answers. It got scared and lost. At one stage we stopped questioning it and started abusing it!!

At the conclusion of this part of the video, the group were beginning to notice that Dak was becoming weaker and more silent, and that their voices were gaining strength. As Shannon describes:

After a while Dak started losing some of its power and it didn't like that. The other's voices got stronger and stronger. By the end, Dak didn't have the power.

The group asked that we commence our next session by reviewing this section of video, so that they could see the changes in positioning and the gaps that were opening up for a different story to emerge.

Reviewing the dialogue

When we commenced again after a two-week holiday break, I expected that there would have been some changes within the group, and feared that holidays, boredom, peer pressure and other factors could have provided space for Dak to regain its strong voice in some lives. The group gathered and we talked about the holiday break. Two students reported that Dak had lured them back, but both said that they'd felt 'so stink' after a session that they had been able to refuse after that. Other group members who stated that they had 'kicked Dak' were all pretty proud of themselves. Some talked about being 'unsure' how long they could keep Dak at bay, and others said that they'd never 'let it control' their lives again. They talked about whether they could use and be 'in control' and expressed concern over the fact that Dak was so deceitful that it could trick them into thinking that they were in control when they might not be. All group members had taken to having 'externalising conversations' about Dak.

They asked to see the video, which they reviewed from the beginning, and afterwards the two people who had played the part of Dak asked if they could ask some questions of the group, remaining in the role of Dak. I did not know where this was going to lead, so asked that they check out if it was appropriate with the group, all of whom consented. This seemed to be a big mistake, because it gave Dak back a voice, and with this voice these students, in a taunting and dramatic way (which I now know they had pre-planned), asked questions about why the group would let them speak in their lives. They asked about what these users had expected of Dak, and laughed mockingly at some suggestions like, 'I'd hoped that I could use you without becoming addicted to you', 'I am in control, you're not', 'I hoped you would help me control anger', 'I thought if you helped me control nervousness, I'd get through School Certificate', 'You bring me friends', and 'My mates think I'm cool when I'm stoned'.

These two students then asked if they could 'de-role'; whether they could lead two groups in a discussion about what had just been said; how they had felt in their roles as Dak; and how the others had felt during the interviewing. Again, the rest of the group agreed and a hearty discussion took place about how they can actively support each other in 'overcoming Dak'. I wished that I had been able to video this session, as it highlighted for me the possibilities of extending the characters involved in the conversation. The vitality of the conversation brought home to me the importance of creating a wider audience to such conversations as they could be an invaluable resource which could be used in other areas of our school (i.e. in subjects such as health, life skills, social studies).

Conclusion

I wouldn't say that the conversations we had made everyone stop smoking Dak but it changed the way we talked about it. Some of us had already stopped, others of us still smoke a bit. If adults tried to have these sorts of conversations it wouldn't work so well. The reason it worked was because we can relate to other students. It was great that there was such a mixture of people. It wasn't just all of us Maori, there were Maori and Pakehas and Samoans and people of different ages. (Amber)

As Amber describes, the conversations we shared seemed to enable a different way of thinking about and talking about Dak. What made this possible? When I presented these notes to the group to check with them the accuracy of what I had written, they discussed the importance to them of investigating and interviewing the problem to find out all they could about it, and then in reviewing this part of video. It was as they watched this video that they noticed 'shifts' in the ways they were thinking.

They asked me if I thought all 'problems' would be so 'arrogant' and wondered if this process would work if they were to interview other problems. They also talked about how important it was to them that the two people who had chosen to play in the role of Dak were strong members of the group who had a lot of knowledge about Dak. They said that when they noticed them becoming defeated and withdrawn, they knew they were beginning to beat Dak. I asked them if they would find videos with people interviewing problems a good way of learning, and they responded that they would - as long as the process was student-directed.

They asked me what I thought of interviewing 'different cultures' not as problems, but as ways of making meaning from a 'safe' outsider's point of view. Some said that this process would be useful in such situations because they would not feel guilty about things that they did not know and felt that they could not ask. It seems that there is an unlimited potential for the use of these externalising conversational processes within school settings. In terms of Dak, there remains a powerful determination to continue to expose its influence and methods in Melville High School, as Puni explains:

I don't know what Dak would think about the fact that it is being exposed now. I don't know what it would think about how the stuff we talked about is now being written down! Dak's a pretty quiet thing. It often makes people hide and lie about it. I've never ever seen Dak be exposed as much as we exposed it. So I don't know what will happen now.

Tennessey was in our group. We knew he'd been a pretty hard-core druggy. He was really determined to give it up. I think he was really, really hooked. He was depressed and so sad. When he was telling us that he'd said 'no' to Dak it meant a lot. Tennessey thought it was important to talk about Dak. He felt strongly about it. I think he'd really like it that we're still talking about it and talking about him. He'd want us to expose Dak. I believe he's with us as we do it. But we have to remember it doesn't always make life easier or better when you stand against something powerful and your mates.

Notes

1. First published in the 1998 Nos.2&3 *Dulwich Centre Journal*. Republished here with permission.
2. For those readers interested in further explorations on talking about drug use please refer to Moss, P. & Butterworth, P. (1999), *MOSAIC: An alternative resource for working with young people around drug use* (Dulwich Centre Publications), and 'New perspectives on addiction', *Dulwich Centre Newsletter*, Nos.2&3, 1997 (special issue).
3. Kathy, Puni, Shannon & Amber can be contacted c/- Melville High School, PO Box 3107, Hamilton, New Zealand.

2

Interviewing Racism[1]

by

Donald McMenamin[2]

My response to reading about and thinking about the externalising conversations with problems undertaken in Malawi and Australia around HIV/AIDS, Diabetes and Grief[3] was to wonder how these ways of working could be employed in a school setting. Initially I wondered if we could work on 'mocking try-hard' - the attitude that it is not cool to make efforts towards excellence in the classroom. However, in response to a situation that occurred, I decided to look at the role of 'Racism' in our school.

The idea was simple enough - we could set up an interview with Racism. We wondered how best to do this and thought about the idea of a role-play which then developed into the idea of developing a short drama. I approached Eric Bernard, the drama teacher, with the idea and he was enthusiastic. We called a lunch-time meeting of his third form drama class. Here we presented the idea of externalizing a problem and interviewing it, and outlined the sort of areas we would be curious about, using Roth & Epston (1996) as a guide. The group then brainstormed Racism's responses to these questions and a script of three acts was quickly generated.

At the same time I had been exploring other methods of communicating these ideas. I approached a group of sixth form acapela singers in the school wondering if they would be interested in writing and performing music in ways

13

that externalized 'Racism'. They were keen and wrote a song of four verses. These verses were performed between the three acts of the drama, providing a richness and a sense of continuity between acts.

The group met over a number of lunch-times to practice the drama. Costumes were prepared - coloured masks for race groups, a cowl for 'Racism', set pieces for actors like cards, rugby ball, etc. A sixth form video studies group needed something to video for their class assessments, and they were drawn-in to provide a three-camera edited video of 'Interviewing Racism'.

This play was a first foray for me into the area of drama. I learnt a great deal about the mechanics of organising students and managing a script. The drama teacher, Eric, (without whose expertise the project would not have advanced) and I decided to continue with the idea of using school drama groups to address problems within the school. Eric is enthusiastic about using the skills of senior drama groups to explore these ideas more fully and to present them to wider audiences (e.g. school assemblies).

These ways of working have the potential to engage drama groups, drama teachers, video studies classes, and ready-made audiences at assemblies in the discussion of 'community issues'. They seem ideally suited for school settings. I am very interested in Gerald Monk's (personal communication, 1997) idea of producing a script, putting on the play, getting feedback from the school, incorporating this feedback in the next script, and developing an ongoing conversation in this way. That seems to be the next step! The script developed by the group follows.

Interviewing Racism

Scene I

Lights come up on singing group on a small riser. They sing the song *Racism* by Dylan Regler:

> *Why do we fight?*
> *Why can't we get along?*
> *Let's do what's right*
> *Let's replace what went wrong*

> *The future is near and our kids live in fear*
> *So why don't we change?*
> *Leave the past, live again.*

As lights come up it becomes clear that there are many masked actors on stage, each representing a racial group, indicated by a different primary colour. On the right there are two characters talking. On the left two characters are playing chess. In the centre two characters are throwing a rugby ball. And at the back of the stage four characters are playing cards around a table. Racism enters from the right.

> Racism points to the two characters talking with each other: *Hate!*
> They stop talking and turn their backs on each other.
> Racism moves to the two playing rugby: *Hate!*
> They stop playing and one of the boys throws the ball violently at the other.
> Racism moves to the card players: *Hate!*
> One of the actors collects the cards and they disperse.
> Racism moves on to the chess players: *Hate!*
> They stop playing.
> Racism points to the audience: *Hate!*

Racism exits on the left and the groups rearrange themselves along racial lines. Everyone exits making gestures at one another.

Scene II: The Interview

Lights up on singing group:

> *Isn't it time for us to change?*
> *Time for us to rearrange?*
> *The problems that we've made*
> *The controversy got to end*
> *Time for us to make amend*
> *Of the problems that we've made*

As lights come up it becomes clear the stage is the set of a talk show. Racism stands on the left-hand side behind a table. Two interviewers are seated on the right-hand side behind the table. There are also two functional cameramen on stage.

1st Interviewer: [to camera] *Good day, ladies and gentlemen, and welcome to the 'chat show'. Today we have a very special interview. Our guest has come out of hiding especially for this program - and it is my pleasure to welcome - Racism.*

2nd Interviewer: *This is a one-off opportunity so let's get straight to it, shall we? Racism, the first question we have for you is quite simple - where have you been hiding?*

Racism: *Ah yes, yes, well - hiding - yes - I've been unseen rather than hiding - yes?? Unseen - I've been unseen in lots of places. A long time ago I was unseen in Germany, after that in South Africa. Recently nobody saw me in Bosnia, in Rwanda and in Burundi. You can see where I've been but often people don't realise it's me that's been there - you know? And I've been here at your school for a while but this is the first time I've come out in the open like this.*

1st Interviewer: *So why are you here at our school?*

Racism: *Same old reasons! I want to stop people getting on with each other. I want to split up mixed groups into single race groups. I want conflict, I want jealousy,*
I want fear!!! Yessir - that's why I'm here!

2nd Interviewer: *I don't think the school will fall for that! How do you expect to be able to trick us into that?*

Racism: *Hahahaha! Not fall for that? So long as nobody sees me you'll fall for it, all right! I've got everything on my side - the movies show people in race groups, the newspapers blame races for crimes, the TV does stuff by race groups! All around people are getting divided up by their colours! Well it's too easy! All I have to do is get those groups to stop trusting each other - to stop talking to each other - and BINGO - next thing we've got conflict, we've got jealousy - we've got fear!! Excellent!!*

1ˢᵗ Interviewer: *Sounds like you've got some help in your plans - some friends on your side!*

Racism: *Well - not friends exactly. Let's say there are lots of people who help me without really meaning to!!! (I prefer not to have friends!) So the TV helps me, radio and newspapers help me. They don't mean to - but they do anyway! Also - anytime I can trick a group of people into not trusting another group - that helps me too! So - yes - I do get help! That's part of the fun of it for me - tricking people into helping me!*

2ⁿᵈ Interviewer: *Is there anyone or anything that does not help you?*

Racism: *Oh yes - curse their eyes! Oh yes. No matter where I go there are always some people who can see me. If I can shut them up it's okay. If I can make them look silly or stupid it's okay. But if people listen to them - if people pay attention to them - ahhh - the game is up for me. I can't win when people see me. Oh yes - curse their eyes - I've got enemies all right!*

1ˢᵗ Interviewer: *These people who can see you - what is it they see and what is it they say about that?*

Racism: *Somehow they can see that my lies aren't true. Somehow they can see that people of different races are actually very much alike - much more alike than I want them to see. And when they talk to people of different races they find out that they are often interested in the same sort of things. I hate it! How can I split people up when they have common interests. And they talk about it. Loudmouths - why can't they keep their mouths shut? I want people to believe that different races have nothing to say to each other. Damn their eyes!*

2ⁿᵈ Interviewer: *Well that's very interesting. And apart from people who see you, does anything else stand in your way?*

Racism: *Yes, yes, dammit - I hate that sport. When people play sport together they mix up the race groups I've been working so hard to get going. And then they talk to each other. And they have fun. I hate it when people have fun. Yes - I'd say that sport is a real problem to me!*

2ⁿᵈ Interviewer: *Well Racism - this has certainly been an eye-opener for me. I* *can't help wondering if you haven't made a mistake by coming on our program and letting all these people see you. However, thank you very much for coming out of hiding and providing such an interesting interview.*

Racism: *I'm not coming back here ...*

Scene III

Lights up on singing group:

> *Will the people's racism be clear?*
> *Will they have to live in fear?*
> *Maybe the noises you hear*
> *Could be a voice in your ears*
> *Racism is near*
> *Be careful, be strong, be aware*

As lights come up it becomes clear that the scene is the same as it was at the end of Scene I. Characters are in separate groups based on colour. Racism goes up to the first group.

> Racism: *Hate!*
> The group stands together: *No!*
> Racism stumbles and turns to the next group: *Hate!*
> The group stands together: *No!*
> Racism stumbles and turns to the next group: *Hate!*
> The group stands together: *No!*

Racism stumbles and staggers and finally falls. The separate groups come together, collect around him, and pull off his cape. With his cape removed it is clear he is wearing the same clothes as the others. Collectively they hold the cape up in the air.

ALL: *There was nobody there. It was all just a trick after all.*

As the cape is held together in the air the singing begins again for the last time:

Now you've seen the pain it's caused
And you've seen how it went wrong
Long before the children were born
But it's time they learn to fight this war
Let live, as one people
The world, is one people

THE END!

Notes

1. First published in the 1998 Nos.2&3 *Dulwich Centre Journal*. Republished here with permission.
2. Donald can be contacted c/- Hillcrest High School, PO Box 11020, Hamilton, New Zealand.
3. See:

   '*Pang'ono pang'ono ndi mtolo* - little by little we make a bundle. The work of the *CARE Counsellors & Yvonne Sliep*' (1998). In White, C. & Denborough, D. (eds), *Introducing Narrative Therapy: A collection of practice-based writings*, Chapter 8. Adelaide: Dulwich Centre Publications.

   Wingard, B. 1998: 'Introducing "sugar".' In White, C. & Denborough, D. (eds), *Introducing Narrative Therapy: A collection of practice-based writings*, Chapter 9. Adelaide: Dulwich Centre Publications

   Wingard, B. 1998: 'Grief: Remember, reflect, reveal.' In White, C. & Denborough, D. (eds), *Introducing Narrative Therapy: A collection of practice-based writings*, Chapter 10. Adelaide: Dulwich Centre Publications

PART II

Group
Work

3

Sharing the load:
Group conversations
with young Indigenous men [1]

by

Ashley Couzens [2]

*As a twenty-four year old Indigenous Australian man, I have a
passion for mental health awareness in Aboriginal communities
and self-empowering others to make decisions over their lives. Over
the last three years I've worked as an Aboriginal Mental Health
Worker within various South Australian communities including:
Raukkan, Meningie, Murray Bridge, the Riverland and Adelaide.
The groups talked about in this paper were run in the Riverland
and Meningie.*

My passion for working with young Indigenous men started right back at high
school. When I was at school there wasn't much support for us Indigenous men
around mental health issues. And yet the years between 12 and 18 are so
crucial.

During these years, Indigenous young men are trying to find their way in the world in the context of so many changes - not only with their own body but in the environment and the community around them. Finding a place to fit, to belong, is a huge issue. For a lot of young Australian men coming of age is a time of isolation. When racism and the loss of Aboriginal cultural identity is also involved it can be pretty hard to find your fit with the broader community. There's a lot of weight on these young guys' shoulders. Fitting in with your peers has a different meaning when your elders are dying out at such a rapid rate; your culture, although rebuilding, has been devastated; and when suicide is slowly eating away at your connections and families.

It's within this context that I facilitate groups for young Indigenous guys in schools. I'm employed as one of only two Aboriginal Adolescent mental health workers in South Australia. The groups we run are an opportunity for young Indigenous men to have some different sorts of conversations, to share the load. Why see a kid individually when they've got the same hassles as six or ten other kids in the same school? Aboriginal young people are really fearful of clinical ways of counselling. They find it really hard to understand what the counsellor is saying and where they are coming from. Talking and yarning in a group however is a part of Aboriginal life, it's something they can relate to.

Before the groups begin I consult with the school and the local community about what sorts of issues they believe would be important to create space to discuss. This varies from place to place however what I call the 'main players' are always around - drugs & alcohol, suicide & grief, and racism & aggression. These issues always crop up.

But before I talk about the 'main players' let me share with you the secrets of our 'bench system' which derives from Aussie Rules Football. Football is really significant in these young guys lives. It's role models like Andrew McLeod who spur these kids on (for those of you who aren't from Australia Andrew McLeod is an Aboriginal football star).

The bench system came out of collaboration with the first group I ran. When I asked them how they'd like to keep the group on track they said they'd like to have a footy bench system. We sat down and tossed around some ideas and worked it out, and it went from there. I use it in every group now because it really works.

Each week one student is the designated umpire. If one of the kids breaks one of the ground rules (which have all been established by the group) then the umpire gives the student a warning. For a second break of the rules the student is sent off - benched, in the sin-bin, for ten or so minutes. The group decides the time. When they come back into the group and apologise, we talk about what happened, what made him feel angry or what sort of sparked him off. If there's a third breakage of the rules then the student has a meeting with the Aboriginal Education Workers, myself, and the principal. But this hardly ever needs to happen. We develop a team game sort of feel and it works fantastically.

Most of the boys play football, they relate to it and respect it. Football for many is a form of therapy. If you can channel your rage into sport and use it the right way that's a form of therapy. We try to use the same concept at school. If you get angry at school, and for young Aboriginal guys there's often plenty to be angry about, then you've got to try and channel your anger into different ways, ways that will work. In order to explore how to do this we often experiment with role plays.

Role plays

Dealing with racism and aggression is an everyday experience for young Aboriginal guys. Finding ways to have conversations about this seems important. We do some role plays on aggression and racism. For example, someone plays the role of a shopkeeper. A young guy might walk into the shop and he gets stared at, watched like a hawk. The shopkeeper's thinking he's going to steal something. The kids had great fun in this role play. We explored how you could respond by actually approaching the shopkeeper and saying that you felt uncomfortable and you're going to contact the Equal Opportunity Commission. That was kind of the right way. After having practiced that they also got a chance to do the wrong way, sticking their fingers up, saying 'piss off. I'm getting out of here', and knocking over a trolley or something! The other group members who were watching had to pick which was the right way to take control of the situation. I think everyone just wanted to do the wrong way sometimes, they had so much fun with it! They don't usually get the chance to swear that loudly in school!

We also role-played schoolyard situations like getting bumped at the tap and how you can control yourself. That was funny. I had some kids lined up and drinking out of the taps and one guy would come along and bump them all like dominoes. Then they'd try and figure out how they could respond.

We had great conversations about identifying the signs that can occur before you get angry, like your face might get hot, your hands might sweat, little signs like that. It just teaches them to say look out, I'm getting hot in the face, I'm starting to get worked up, what am I going to do? A lot of the young guys were unaware that they had any rights at all in these situations. There's so many little things that can generate rage when you're a young Indigenous man. I think it's because the lads feel so powerless to do anything about them that they get frustrated. Having these conversations can create a different understanding of what they are going through. They can share the load with each other, look out for each other.

Drugs and alcohol

In trying to talk about the issue of alcohol and drugs it seems important to clarify that I don't believe that Indigenous people's abuse drugs and alcohol any more so than non-Indigenous Australians. Aboriginal people basically drink the same as other Australians - it's just in different, more public settings. That said, issues of drugs and alcohol are really important to talk about. Generally speaking, although not all the young guys in the group may have used alcohol and /or other drugs they will all have been closely involved with it.

How to talk about drugs and alcohol needs thoughtfulness. There's often this concept that everything about drugs and alcohol is negative. It's pretty hard to have an interesting conversation if everything is negative! I mean obviously drugs and alcohol are negative for the body, but there are some positive things to talk about too especially in relation to the stands that people have made in relation to alcohol and other drugs, and about how people can care for one another. These are the sorts of things which we focus on in the groups.

We talk a lot about how you can comfort friends who might be using, what are the different ways and techniques you can use to approach a friend without being too straightforward or too harsh. People get the chance to share their ideas and skills with one another. Often these conversations are quite beautiful.

Grief

Grief and suicide is an enormously important area to talk about. In one of the groups we moved the topic of grief up to week three because there were three deaths in the community in the first three weeks - one of them was a suicide. The kids were really feeling the brunt of it. There is often a massive rippling effect whenever an event happens in the community, like a death or an arrest. The effects flow right through the families, down the line to the children who will feel the effects but often don't know how to respond.

We talk about grief and the little things that people can do to comfort parents, uncles, aunties. There's not much a young guy can do but we really acknowledge the little things that the young guys are already doing, like making mum and dad a coffee, or doing special things around the house. They have told us that it helps to know that their contributions are being honoured. They also get new ideas from each other.

Often I don't think the school knows how much deaths in the community really affect the kids. Aboriginal people have a different sense of family, of community than non-Aboriginal people, so someone who is not blood related may absolutely be family. If they die there is a sense of collective grief. If they are due to suicide the grief can be heartbreaking.

We asked the last group as a whole if they had known someone who had committed suicide or someone who had tried and ten of the fourteen kids said they had - most of them were family members. Suicide in the Aboriginal community is 300 times higher than in the non-Aboriginal community. That's just appalling. And it's not just loss of family, it's loss of land and loss of language that makes grief one of the major issues in the Aboriginal community.

Conversations about grief and suicide can be pretty hard. I find it hard not to break down myself with some of the stories I've heard. Although it is a hard topic, and I'm relieved when it's over, I feel good to know that the young guys have had a chance to share what's going on for them, and to share a few little things to take home to try to be helpful. It makes them feel a little bit safer in a way that they've got a couple of ideas in their head of how they can support their family if it happens again.

Language

Language and life go hand-in-hand. Without your own language there comes a profound loss of identity. Ngarrindjeri language gives these guys a real sense of belonging. We used to go out into the communities to the elders and research it, try to find words that we may have missed. We got a lot of stuff on tape and now within the groups we spend a bit of time teaching language to the younger guys. In the groups we ask the kids to come up with a sentence or two to say to their partner. They had lists of words in front of them and they started having a go at each other with sentences like 'you've got big emu ears' or 'you've got a wombat foot' and stuff like that! It was really fun. There were a lot of one liners coming out in Ngarrindjeri language. Teaching language is fantastic. Once you start learning you've got to know more.

Building connections

When I first approach a school to offer to facilitate a group for the Aboriginal guys sometimes some of the non Aboriginal on the staff get worried that it's gonna create an 'us and them' situation within the school. Funny thing is, generally there already is an 'us and them' situation in the school. The Aboriginal kids and non-Aboriginal students have virtually segregated themselves from each other - the power of racism is still strong. I'd like to see that segregation changed because when the groups come together it makes non-Aboriginal students so much more aware of cultural issues. If racism is every going to change then that's really important.

As part of the program we do an activity in the last couple of weeks called 'breaking down barriers'. Each Aboriginal student in the group picks a non-Aboriginal student in the school who they aren't really familiar with, to do a profile on. They choose their kids and I ask the teachers if these kids could be released for say half an hour. During this time all the young guys sit on a bench or under a tree and the Aboriginal guys do some interviewing to find the things they have in common. It's the little things in common that build the connections - like supporting the same footy teams; or both owning a dog. These little things generate conversation. It's fun for everyone, they really enjoy it. There are a lot of laughs. You can hear the Aboriginal guys yelling 'shame job, shame job', but they really enjoy it. They list the things they have in common. When we have our presentation the profiles are placed on a display board with their photo, arm-in-arm with a non-Aboriginal kid. The Aboriginal kids start walking around a bit more and talk to other kids which is really good to see.

I love these groups. They bring me a sense of hope. There wasn't much support around for us when we were at school. That's got to change. These groups are just one starting point. They are trying to reclaim a sense of self-empowerment of young people. Hopefully this can then ripple outwards into the communities.

Notes

1. First published in the 1998 Vol.3 *Gecko*. Republished here with permission
2. Ashley can be contacted c/- Dulwich Centre Publications, Hutt St PO Box 7192, Adelaide 5000, South Australia.

4

The journey of a lifetime:

Group work with young women who have experienced sexual assault[1]

by

Lisa McPhie & Chris Chaffey[2]

Background

The Sexual Assault Support Service in Hobart, Tasmania, Australia, has a long history of running various kinds of groups for adult women survivors of sexual assault. Largely as a result of hearing back from women, the Service has long recognised the immense benefits of groups in breaking down isolation, normalising feelings and behaviours, providing a witness group to women's stories, and creating a strong sense of solidarity as women stand up to the effects of sexual abuse.

In 1995 we began to realise that perhaps it would be useful to develop a group for the large number of young women who were accessing the Service. Often these young women would contact the Service at times of crisis, and then disappear for months until the next crisis. As workers we began to wonder whether one-to-one counselling was meeting the needs of some of these young women. Although they would say they felt comfortable using the Service and that it was beneficial to them, as workers it was frustrating that each crisis seemed to be a re-run of the previous one. There seemed little opportunity to have conversations with the young women that might in any way lessen the powerful legacies from their experiences of sexual abuse and the crises that were ensuing. We also wondered if the relatively formal structures of one-to-one counselling were in some way off-putting to many of these young women. We wondered if this was why they would access counselling only in desperate times.

Through our conversations with individual young women, it became clear that many of them were struggling with similar issues: isolation, fear, self-hate, overwhelming sadness at loss of family, and the blaming of themselves for the abuse they had experienced. It also became very apparent that they all had much wisdom to offer. The potential benefits of providing a context in which they could connect with each other became more clear.

As a result of these conversations, we began to facilitate a young women's group. We hoped to provide a space in which young women could come together to talk about issues in an informal way. It was hoped that meeting together in a group would break down the intense isolation and feelings of 'being different' that many of the young women were experiencing. It was also hoped that the group would provide a way in which some of the young women could keep in regular contact with the Service. For us as facilitators there was a strong sense of hope that if a context could be created for conversations to happen now, then perhaps the legacies of sexual assault wouldn't still be dominating these women's lives in years to come.

We began with an open group program based on a series of information sessions around safety, self-care, self-harm, fear, anger, relationships, and other issues related to the effects of sexual abuse on people's lives. In hindsight, we wonder how useful these sessions were. Our own tentativeness at imposing any structure, and our own fear of asking too much of the participants, resulted in the sharing of lots of food, laughter and fun, but not much dialogue around the issues of surviving sexual assault. Still, it was a beginning.

We then decided to change the group format completely and use more of a narrative approach. What we ended up with was a closed group that ran one evening a week for ten weeks. Each group session was two hours long. We also held a weekend camp in the seventh week. We based much of the format and content of the group sessions on the 'Discoveries' program developed by Sheridan Linnell and Dorothy Cora (1993).

This group proved much more useful from both our perspective and the perspective of the participants. The comments from the group participants were extremely positive with threats of a 'sit in' if the Service even contemplated not running another young women's group. Our experience of facilitating this group and being with the young women, especially during the weekend camp, inspired enthusiasm for future groups and generated many ideas as to what these groups might look like.

These ideas gradually took shape to form the 'journey of a lifetime' group. This paper describes this group, the content of the sessions, the experiences of the young women, and our experiences as facilitators. As well as describing the groups, we've also included some of the documents that are involved in this 'journey'. Like many journeys, the 'journey of a lifetime' involves tickets, passports, travel books which describe some of the hazards and deceptions of travelling through difficult terrain, and writing letters home. Like other journeys, it also requires a map - which doubles as our group flyer (see over page).

The flyer

In previous groups we had witnessed how powerful the use of metaphors and analogies could be. Within previous groups, conversations often likened the women's stories to the process of a journey. The young women had found that having an image of themselves as travellers roller-blading on a bendy highway, or like certain characters (real life or fictional) was an important way that they could use to stay connected to who they wanted to be. Thus we wanted to create a flyer that captured some of the spirit and excitement of starting out on a journey. We hoped that the idea of a treasure map would ignite people's curiosity, and promote the idea that the group might lead them to undiscovered treasures. The concept of a journey also appealed to us as we felt that it conveyed the idea that looking at issues in one's life is not a smooth, linear path; that it can often be hard work and involve travelling backwards and forwards between places. We have spoken with many young women who have

• 6 Pulling yourself out of the quicksand of self-hate

GREAT

clu

RIVER

THIS WAY

• 7 Holding onto hope in the face of fear and terror

AIR MAIL PAR AVION
12 Australia Post

• 8 Letting everyone know where I really am

Rehashing the trip and looking at the photos

• 9 and 10

It's really good being a girl

can be wonderful

• 11 Too much of a good thing

4 Trusting your instincts in the forest of deception

5 caping the guilt es of the guilt andits

2 Rewriting the book of tricks, lies & bullshit

3 Leaving behind the burden of secrecy

1 Daring to say hello to the travel brochure of dreams

12 Saying oodbye to the group and continuing on with the journey

experienced sexual assault who have told us how they feel as if their lives will always be captured by the effects of sexual abuse. Visually we wanted the flyer to convey a sense of hope and possibilities.

Deciding on the topics

The decision about which topics to include in the twelve weeks was a difficult one to make. After talking with many young women about various ways to structure the program we decided to have all the topics mapped out before the group started. This was because the feedback we had received from young women was that they felt much less apprehensive about coming to a group when they knew what the topic was going to be. Many young women said that it was scary enough just to come to a group, and that if they had not had some idea of what the conversations would be about then they would not have felt confident enough to attend. In response to this feedback, we decided on structuring the topics in advance and discussing at the start of each week what that session would entail.

Despite these decisions to have a fixed structure, we wanted the groups to be flexible. A considerable amount of time throughout the program was spent talking with the group about how useful they thought the group topics were and whether we needed to be doing things differently. During the twelve weeks the group members did come up with other topics they would like to discuss but felt that these extra topics would be ideas for a future group, as they wanted the current program to stay as planned.

The actual decision of which topics to include was based on our experience of one-to-one counselling with young women. In those conversations the most common themes centred around issues pertaining to secrecy, self-blame, self-doubt, self-loathing, and fear. Thus we decided to include these topics in the group sessions. As the group was going to be a closed group where many of the participants would not know each other, we also felt it was important to have an introductory session and a goodbye party at the end. We included a session that looked at some of the community attitudes they had faced, and what they had been told or had heard about sexual assault. This, to us, seemed an essential topic to include so that the young women would have the opportunity to contextualise their experiences. The rest of the topics involved experimenting with using letters and reflective teams within the group. We hoped that these would be ways for the group to connect and honour each other. We hoped that acknowledgement from each other would be more powerful than anything we as facilitators could offer.

The group members

The group consisted of seven young women whose ages ranged from 14-24. They were an extremely diverse group in terms of their socio-economic backgrounds, current living situations, and current lifestyles. They were all survivors of childhood sexual abuse and some had experienced more recent sexual assaults. Three of the seven group members were quite familiar with the Service as they had been using it for one-to-one counselling. For the others the group was their first contact with the Service, having been given flyers from workers in other agencies.

The group program - outlines

The following outlines describe the main themes for each week and some of the focus questions we used to start discussions. They do not do justice to the conversational nature of the group and need to be read more as reference points for conversations. They were often the starting point from which we tried to initiate re-authoring conversations. Sometimes these conversations happened as one large group, sometimes in pairs or small groups. We have not included here the introductory exercises we used with the group each week.

Week 1: Daring to say hello to the travel brochure of dreams

After thorough introductions, the first week involved speaking about the flyer, the outline of the group and introducing the concept of the journey. We explored group agreements, expectations in relation to commitments to the group and, where appropriate, structured in support for people between the groups. We then gave out a handout about 'Hopes and Fears' which we asked participants to fill in and then discuss in small groups. Then we came back into the big group and explored the question, 'What hopes and fears do we have in common?' We found that this in some way created a sense of common ground between participants and seemed to help participants feel a sense of support from one another.

In the second half of the first group meeting we introduced the metaphor of a journey. As discussed earlier, we have found in our conversations with young women that such a metaphor conveys a sense of movement and possibilities - even when the journey is at times difficult. Throughout the group, right from sending out the flyer, we had many concerns about how the young women would relate to the metaphors and externalisations we planned to use in the weekly sessions. We did not want to present these analogies as being rigid or as being the only ways to understand particular problems. Rather, we hoped to present them as tools or starting points to assist the young women to develop their own understandings of the problems they were up against. We hoped that by using various metaphors and analogies the result would be a greater separation from the problem for the young women involved in the group. Our experience has been that it is so much easier for people to see and/or to move in the direction that they prefer when they have a clear view of what is getting in the way.

Throughout the group sessions the metaphors and analogies were presented much more tentatively than the written word conveys. We spent some time each session checking out if a particular image fitted with the participants' experience and what words they had used to describe what we were talking about. We often ended up with a variety of metaphors and names for problems.

We asked the group members to consider where and when they started this journey. We asked questions like:

- *What was the starting place like?*
- *What did it look like?*
- *What did it feel like?*
- *What would you call it?*
- *Where are you now?*
- *What does it feel like here?*

- *What would you call this place where you are now?*
- *Where is this journey taking you - the place where you want to be?*
- *What will this place look like?*
- *What will you be like?*
- *What will be different about your life?*
- *What will it feel like to be where you want to be at last?*
- *How will you get from where you are to where you want to be?*
- *What personal strengths will help you keep moving forward?*
- *What might trip you up, get in your way, force you to stub your toe as you move forward?*
- *What is it about you that will help you to get around these obstacles?*

We have found that often it is helpful to provide some metaphors or ideas to get participants started. We often liken the journey as similar to being in a tunnel - describing the sense that it will never end, that they don't know what is coming next, and that sometimes it feels like the tunnel is closing in on them.

After speaking about this, we asked the group members to use paper, coloured pens , crayons, magazines and other things to represent the journey that they are on. And we asked them to give their work a title. We then invited a large group discussion in which each person shared their representation or title with the group.

One young woman drew an elaborate map that resembled something like a street directory. The street names were things like 'Secret Circle' and 'Unworthiness Street'. She was on her way to a place called 'Nearly Home', and described where she was at present as being on a road to 'Nearly Home' that had a large sign that said 'No U-Turns'. Another young woman described her journey as being about a quest for a secret love, which was a love for herself.

We followed this up by asking each person to name a skill, some piece of knowledge that they have accumulated, or a strength, that helps them to keep moving forward. The following questions then acted as a basis for a group 'brainstorm':

- *Having glimpsed what's at the end of the tunnel, how might this group help you to keep moving along towards this?*

- *Are there other group agreements we need to add?*

Some of the responses to how the group might 'help you to keep moving along' included: support, encouragement, sharing thoughts, providing hope, security, being here, knowing I'm not the only one, and being inspired by other people's journeys.

To end the first week, we invited reflections about the meeting and about what it meant to each person that they attended the group.

Week 2: Rewriting the book of tricks, lies and bullshit

The focus for this session was to try to create a space in which the young women could contextualise their experiences of sexual assault. After a group round responding to the question, 'Was it harder or easier to stand up to the fear of coming here tonight?', we tried to invite conversations that would articulate the broader context of the young women's experience of abuse. We invited a group brainstorm that was written up on a whiteboard, orientated around the following questions:

- *What are some of the ideas that people have about women and girls who have been sexually abused?*
- *How might these ideas affect women?*
- *Which of these ideas have pushed you around the most?*
- *What are the things that you have heard said about people who sexually abuse women and children?*
- *What have you heard said about mothers of children who have experienced sexual assault?*

We then split the group up into small groups and each small group took one of the above ideas that had pushed them around and discussed the following questions:

- *How did you get this idea?*
- *Who encouraged this idea?*
- *How did they trick you into believing this, i.e., what did they tell you? What did they do?*

-   *Who benefits when this belief pushes you around?*

Participants wrote their discussion points on large pieces of paper and we stuck these lists to the wall. We then went back into the large group to discuss everyone's reaction to reading the lists.

After a short break we then introduced the 'book of tricks, lies, and bullshit' to the group. We explored the idea that often tricks and lies are presented as the truth, and that part of the journey to escape from the effects of sexual abuse is to identify the tricks, lies and bullshit in order to make sense of one's own experience. We checked with participants if this fitted for them - and it did. We talked with the participants about making up a book that listed some of the 'tricks, lies, and bullshit', a book that could be continually updated. We asked the participants if they thought that some of the information that had come out of the earlier group brainstorm was part of the 'tricks, lies, and bullshit'. The young women agreed, and we then typed into the book the responses to the questions we discussed earlier (i.e. 'What are some of the ideas that people have about women and girls who have been sexually abused?' 'What are the things that you have heard said about people who sexually abuse women and children?' and, 'What have you heard said about mothers of children who have experienced sexual assault?').

We found that this 'book of tricks, lies and bullshit' in some way demystified the experiences of the young women and assisted them to understand how they had been recruited into confusion and self-blame.

Breaking from tricks and lies

In order to create a context in which the young women could identify times in which they had broken from the tricks and lies that cloud experiences of sexual abuse, we asked each participant to think of the first time that they had an inkling that some of what they had been conned into believing was untrue. We asked the group members to discuss in pairs the following questions:

-   *How were you able to recognise and step away from the tricks, lies and bullshit?*
-   *What kinds of things did you have to do, or tell yourself, to step away from the tricks?*

THE BOOK OF TRICKS, LIES AND BULLSHIT

WHAT IT SAYS ABOUT

WOMEN AND GIRLS WHO HAVE BEEN SEXUALLY ABUSED

- If you speak out you ruin the family name
- they asked for it
- what they were wearing ...
- if people knew they wouldn't go out with you
- they are making it up/lying
- if you go to court it will make it worse
- they are exaggerating
- counselling will make it worse
- it's the way they acted, e.g. kissed someone, went somewhere
- forget it now
- they are crazy
- they are bad anyway
- it's your fault ... because
- she's a slut
- she was drunk/stoned
- you have had sex with him before, what's the difference
- she didn't say no, she didn't fight, scream, shout, etc.
- it's a woman's role
- she should have told straight away
- they are damaged for life
- forget about it and it'll go away
- it's every woman's fantasy

WHAT IT SAYS ABOUT
ABUSERS

- he was just breaking her in
- it's normal
- they're sick
- he was confused about his position in the relationship
- he was drunk/drugged
- we should feel sorry for them
- his mother didn't give him enough love
- it won't happen again
- he was abused himself
- they can't control themselves
- he doesn't have any friends
- they didn't understand what they were doing
- it's part of their culture/religion
- all men do this
- he was really old/young
- he's too old to go to court
- don't ruin his name/his life and his family's name/career

WHAT IT SAYS ABOUT
MOTHERS WHOSE CHILDREN ARE SEXUALLY ABUSED

- they didn't do their job properly
- they should know
- didn't she have the intuition to know what was going on
- she didn't banish that person from the family
- she taught her daughter how to be a slut in the first place
- she didn't protect her children
- she left her children in the care of that person

After a time these conversations broadened out to the larger group. We asked further questions:

- *What are some of the ways you have avoided stepping in the bullshit?*
- *How have you been able to start to develop your own shitometer?*

Some of the ways in which the young women have resisted the tricks and lies included: 'listening to the little voice inside me that said everything was not okay', 'realising I need help and acting on that', 'reading the Courage to Heal', 'having willpower', 'being honest to myself', 'allowing myself to have feelings', 'not putting off my happiness', 'coming to the group', 'telling myself that speaking out can't be worse than the abuse', 'constantly saying to myself that my thoughts are as important as others', 'telling myself that people are responsible for their own actions - it's not my fault'.

Before we finished the second meeting of the group a final round took place reflecting on people's experience of the session.

Week 3: Leaving behind the burden of secrecy.

In this week we wished to explore how secrecy can often permeate lots of aspects and areas of people's lives - especially those who have been subject to sexual abuse. In our consultations with young women this has been identified as a very important issue to talk about. The following questions informed the discussions in the group:

- *How do families and society encourage secrecy, especially in children?*
- *How does society / families react to anyone who doesn't play the secrecy game?*
- *Who benefits from secrecy?*

As facilitators we tried to discuss secrecy in terms of the different feelings around 'exciting' secrets that are about fun, pleasure, and closeness; and 'scary' or 'yucky' secrets that betray closeness. We explored how often the latter can become a burden.

In small groups we invited discussions about the following questions, and asked participants to write their responses on large sheets of paper:

- *Have there been times when secrecy has burdened your life? For example, what habits has secrecy recruited you into?*
- *Who has encouraged secrecy in your life and how? For example, by isolating you, or setting you up so that you feel unable to talk to those closest to you.*
- *What fears support secrecy?*

Back in the large group we discussed any similarities that people noticed between each group's responses.

Breaking from secrecy

In order to create space for participants to consider the ways in which the effects of secrecy can be challenged, we invited individual participants to:

Think of a time when secrecy didn't 'steal your voice' and 'strangle your vocal chords', to represent this by using crayons, pens, collage, etc., and then to 'give your work a title'.

Back in the large group we asked participants to share the title or representation with the group. We asked, 'What does it tell you about yourself that you stood up to secrecy on this occasion?' and, 'What one thing would be different about how you treat or think about yourself if you weren't weighed down by the burden of secrecy?'

The young women spoke of how free it would feel to have a choice about whether to keep something a secret or not, how they would be able to actually speak rather than be silenced, and how they could be nicer to themselves if the shame of secrecy wasn't so strong.

Week 4: Trusting your instincts in the forest of deception

In this week we wished to introduce the idea of the 'forest of deception' - a place into which people can be led and from where it is often hard for them to find their way out. The 'forest of deception' is a place in which it is often difficult for people to trust their own sense of reality as there are so many shadows and voices. In our experience of talking with young women who have experienced sexual assault, exploring the metaphor of the 'forest of deception' has enabled a language to be found for the confusion that often accompanies experiences of assault. After briefly introducing the idea of the 'forest of deception' and checking that it fitted for the experience of the young women in the group, we asked the following questions:

- *Who plants the seeds of this confusion and self-doubt?*

- *How do they encourage its growth?*

- *What affect does this forest of deception have on the people who find themselves in it?*

Small group discussions then occurred around further questions:

- *How were you tricked into not trusting yourself and your own reality?*

- *How has this training affected your relationships with others?*

After coming back into the big group, we invited the group members to speak about any similarities that they had noticed in the stories shared in the small groups.

Breaking from deception

In order to illustrate the ways in which the young women had sought to free themselves from the forest of deception, we invited the participants to 'think of a time when you were able to trust your own mind and/or body and not doubt yourself'. We then asked the participants to discuss, in pairs, how they were able to stand up to the training in secrecy and self-doubt, and how they were able to trust themselves on those occasions. We returned to the large group to consider the implications and meanings of these examples. We asked, 'What do these examples of being able to trust yourself tell the group about you?'

Some of the responses of the young women to this question brought forth descriptions of themselves as 'strong', 'courageous', 'someone who could make their own decisions', 'determined', 'persistent' and 'powerful'.

To end the week's discussions we asked participants how the group was going for them. We checked with them whether they felt it was on track and whether we were talking about the sorts of things that they wanted to be talking about.

Week 5: Escaping the clutches of the guilt bandits

In our experience it is very common for young women to feel a degree of responsibility for the assaults that they have been subject to. Within this group session we tried to deconstruct why this is the case. The metaphor of the 'guilt bandits' proved useful in assisting us to do this. Before we introduced the concept of the 'guilt bandits' we asked the following questions:

- *What are some of the tricks and cons that abusers use to deny responsibility for the acts of sexual violence they commit?*
- *In what ways do they try to shift the blame to other people?*

We then introduced the concept of the guilt bandits: bandits that can seem to come from nowhere, who hijack people's thoughts and then leave them feeling confused and captured by guilt. We asked whether the idea of 'guilt bandits' fitted with the young women's experiences, and then asked the following questions:

- *How come the 'guilt bandits' haven't been caught?*
- *Who supports them?*
- *How do they do this?*

We then invited the participants to discuss, in pairs, the following question:

- *When the 'guilt bandits' have you in their clutches what do they tell you about your childhood and/or the abuse to try and keep you from getting away?*

As facilitators we discussed our experience of working with survivors of abuse and assault and how we have often found that women still secretly blame themselves/or feel guilt in relation to some aspect of the sexual abuse. We spoke about how we have often come across the 'guilt bandits' in our conversations with women who have been subject to abuse. We then asked the following questions to the whole group:

- *How active are the 'guilt bandits' in your life?*
- *Do they run wild or are they restricted to certain areas?*

After discussing where the 'guilt bandits' were having an influence and where they were being restricted, we asked each participant in the group to think of a time when they saw the 'guilt bandits' coming and managed to escape. We asked them to consider how they were able to escape their clutches. We invited them to represent this on paper by using words, crayons, collage, etc., and to give their work a title. This was then shared with the whole group. While the representations were being shared we asked two questions:

- *What do you think the rest of the group notice about you that you were able to outsmart the guilt bandits?*
- *If you knew when the 'guilt bandits' were about to appear - what difference would this make in your life?*

We took delight in some of the responses to these questions. The young women articulated that they were 'much more clever than the guilt bandits', that they were 'able to recognise some warning signs that the bandits were around before they were captured', that they were 'fitter than the bandits'. Many of the participants thought that being prepared for the bandits would make a difference as they could remind themselves of the 'tricks, lies, and bullshit' so that when it came out of the bandits' mouths they would recognise it straight away.

We invited the group members to notice during the following week if the 'guilt bandits' tried to sneak up on them.

Week 6: Pulling yourself out of the quicksand of self-hate

This week we wished to introduce the idea of self-hate being like quicksand. Before we did, however, we quickly checked if anyone had bumped into the 'guilt bandits' during the week and, if so, how they had dealt with them. Then we moved onto the topic of self-hate. We spoke of how we believe that babies are not born thinking that they are short, bad, helpless, and damned unfortunate looking. We tried to introduce the idea that the stories we have about ourselves are created in a context, and that, when people experience self-hate, they have often been recruited into these ideas by other people and circumstances. We introduced the idea that self-hate is like a type of quicksand - initially it can be just a bit squishy and uncomfortable, but then you can be sucked right in and feel unable to move. We checked if this description fitted with the young women, and it generally did. In order to expose the origins of self-hate in the lives of the young women, we then asked the following questions:

- *How do you recognise that the quicksand of self-hate is starting to squish up between your toes and block your ears?*
- *What do you find yourself thinking or feeling?*
- *Who leads you into the quicksand in the first place?*
- *How do they do this?*
- *What are some of the messages that society gives to women that sink them further down into the quicksand?*

We then invited the participants, in small groups, to discuss the following questions:

- *How were you tricked into believing you are not an OK person?*
- *How has this self-hate affected your relationship with yourself and others?*

After coming back into one large group, we talked about the things that stood out for people in the small group discussions. We then asked the question:

- *Who gains most when self-hate has control of your life?*

Breaking from self-hate

The previous conversation exposed the quicksand of self-hate for what it is and created a language to describe it. Creating space for participants to break from self-hate was our next aim. We asked participants to think of a time (if even for a second) when they were able to stand up to self-hate and entertain the idea that they might be okay. We asked them to:

- *Think about who would stand with you in knowing that you are an okay person. It might be someone you know now or it might be someone that you knew as you were growing up.*

- *What do/did they see in you that led them to the conclusion that you are an okay person?*

Within a large group discussion we invited conversations about who would stand with each participant in knowing they are 'an okay person'. We asked why these people would stand with them, and the histories of their connection with these people. We evoked the people and the histories within the young women's lives which stand against self-hate and which acknowledge the qualities, skills and knowledges of the young women. We asked further questions including:

- *How can you keep hold of the voice or presence of these people when you are sinking into the quicksand of self-hate?*

- *What kinds of things could you do or say to yourself to stop the quicksand of self-hate sucking you down?*

Some of the responses included: 'talking to the people in my life that know I am okay'; 'reminding myself that I am lovable and that people do care about me'; 'listening to music to drown out the self-hate'; 'doing homework as it feels good to complete something and takes the focus away from the self-hate'; and, 'making time for myself'. One young woman spoke of how she wears a ring that belongs to her grandmother who she feels really loved her for who she was, and how touching the ring is a way of reminding herself that she is lovable.

To complete the night we did a final round orientated to the question, 'What have you learnt about yourself tonight?'

Week 7: Holding onto hope in the face of fear and terror

The focus for this week was fear. In order to catch up with where everyone was at, however, we began this session by asking, 'How have people gone in being able to step around the quicksand of self-hate during the past week?' After a group round on this topic we turned to the issue of fear. We introduced the topic by asking a series of questions:

- *How do we recognise fear?*
- *What happens physically in our bodies?*
- *What is useful/not useful about fear?*
- *What name would you give to the 'unuseful' fear?*

As facilitators, we then introduced the idea that perhaps terror (or whatever name the participants gave to the 'unuseful' fear) was like an unwanted person/companion on their journey. We checked this idea with the young women and they confirmed that terror was like an uninvited traveller who was following them around and seemed to find them even when they didn't want to be found.

We invited participants to discuss the following questions in small groups:

- *When did you first notice that terror became part of your life?*
- *How does terror affect your life?*
- *How does terror affect your relationship with yourself and others?*

We came back together into the large group to discuss the similarities that had been noticed between people's stories.

Breaking from terror

To create space to acknowledge the ways in which the young women were resisting the effects of terror, we asked the following questions.

- *Think of a time when terror wasn't travelling with you.*
- *What was different about this time?*
- *How did you feel?*
- *What were some of the things you felt when terror wasn't with you?*

Within these discussions the word 'hope' was often spoken about. We followed this up by asking the participants, in pairs, to write a definition of hope. We asked:

- *What is hope?*
- *How would you explain it to an alien?*

And then we shared these definitions.

Having done this, we asked about the effects that hope has on terror. In our experience we have found that hope has dramatic effects. At this point, we introduced the idea of the 'Book of Hope'. We invited participants to think about and/or to write their own story of hope. We were very curious about stories of hope. We asked lots of questions:

- *When did you start to recognise you had hope?*
- *What effect has it had in your life?*
- *Are there people who have taught you about hope, or from whom you have borrowed some hope?*
- *What would it be like if you invited hope to become your constant travelling companion?*

Some of the definitions of hope which the young women offered included: 'Hope is the deepest wish from the heart, that was a dream from childhood'; 'Hope is having a reason for going on'. In response to the idea of hope being a constant travelling companion, participants felt they would be 'more able to handle life's ups and downs', that they would feel 'more confident' and 'less scared' about trying things that they don't try now but would like to. They spoke of how it would be exciting and such a relief to travel with hope and not with terror.

Before we ended the group we also discussed with participants how they thought the group was going. We asked about whether they thought it was meeting their expectations. We asked: 'Is it useful?' 'Are the weekly topics relevant?' 'What are we missing out?'

Week 8: Letting everyone know where I really am

To begin the group this week we invited a group round on the following questions:

- *Did anyone invite hope to join them during the week?*
- *Did anyone have further thoughts about hope and the place it has in their journey?*
- *Did anyone think about their story of hope?*

The focus for this week was to enable participants to reflect on their journeys and to catch-up significant people in their lives about how far they had come. As facilitators, we tried to explain the idea of dominant stories and how they can be created and influenced by other people's ideas about us and our lives. We tried to explain the idea that there may be many other stories we all have about ourselves, stories we think are more relevant to who we are or want to be.

We asked the whole group to brainstorm:

- *What are some of the stories you have heard over and over, about yourself?*

Having done this, we invited the participants to think through their journey so far. We asked them to think through where they started out, where they'd been, where they stayed awhile, and the places they'd heard about that they'd like to visit. We invited the participants to recall who they were at the start of their journey and who they were now. We asked the young women to think about some of the places they'd been, like the 'forest of deception', the 'quicksand of self-hate', lugging the burden of secrecy up some huge hill, and the places where the 'guilt bandits' hang out, etc. After inviting them to think this all through we asked the following questions:

- *Now that you can recognise these places, have survived them, and have taken at least one step away from them, what would you tell others about what you have learnt about yourself in the process?*
- *Who might still think you believe the book of bullshit, that you're lost forever in the forest of deception, totally overshadowed by the burden of secrecy, imprisoned by the 'guilt bandits' and over your head in the quicksand of*

self-hate?
- *What would you like to say to these people who have a way out-of-date story of where you are and who you are?*
- *What would you like to say to them to catch them up?*

We invited the participants to spend the next half an hour writing a letter to themselves, to someone else, or to the group, to catch them up on where they were now and what they had come to know about themselves.

After a short break we invited reflections on the process of writing the letters and asked people to read out a sentence, a paragraph, or the whole letter. We asked participants: 'What have you realised about yourself whilst writing the letter?'

At the end of this group we explained how the process of the next two weeks would involve interviewing some of the young women and having the rest of the group act as a reflecting team to their stories. We asked for people to volunteer to be interviewed, or to think about volunteering to be interviewed, about their journey so far.

Weeks 9 & 10: Rehashing the trip and looking at the photos

We began the group this week by asking:
- *How was it during the week thinking about your letter and where you really are at?*
- *Did anyone catch someone up with the information that was in the letter?*

The rest of the session was taken up by interviews of the participants. Each participant who wanted to had a turn to be interviewed by one of the group facilitators. The rest of the group then reflected on what they had heard and were interviewed by the other group facilitator. This process took about 40 minutes. Before we did the first interview we explained carefully the role of the participants who were reflecting.

We felt very apprehensive about how this process would work with the group. Thoughts and worst nightmares were often envisaged in terms of what would be said, whether the group members could stick with the process, what if they found it boring ... and so on. Being now on the other side of the experience, it was definitely a highlight for the participants, and for us. Not all the group members wished to be interviewed which was respected by everyone in the group. The conversations with the individual members were largely about adding more detail and richness to some of the themes that had already come up in the group. One young woman, who had to appear in court the following week, chose to talk about her decision to report the abuse and her worries about going to court, one participant used the time to reflect on the first time she spoke out about the abuse, another talked about her relationship with her family, and others discussed their battles with self-blame and secrecy. One young woman really wanted to be interviewed and, upon starting to have a conversation, found that she was silenced by the intense emotions that speaking up with an audience brought forth. Watching her fight to speak was a really moving experience for all the group, and the group members in the reflecting team were able to powerfully acknowledge this young woman's courage and resilience in being able to get to the point of taking that risk. The comments and conversations that the reflecting teams had were ones that the person being interviewed experienced as respectful and uplifting. Here are some examples of the kinds of things said by team members:

- *How were you able to share it with your friends? 'Cause you had so much horrible stuff happening at home, and all those people trying to alienate you; it was just amazing that you could share it with your friends, that you could trust them.*

- *I haven't got a question but I wrote down some, like, I don't know what you call it, like a positive list. You do what I do. You list everything you do that is good as just being courageous. You've got so many other qualities that are more than being courageous. You're strong, you're enthusiastic, you're definitely open 'cause you got up there first, you're honest about your feelings, you're friendly, and you believe in yourself. All these other things just swamp it being just about courage.*

- *What more does that little voice say? And how do you know to listen to it, and that its right?*

Some of the comments made by the group generally, about the process or their experience of being interviewed were:

- *It was right before going to court. Made me feel so strong to share how far I'd come.*
- *When I get really scared I'll remember the group, and know that you are all with me.*
- *I'm in awe of myself as I look back on my journey and see all the changes.*
- *I felt so inspired.*
- *Felt more connected to the group.*
- *The group's strength, courage, and positive energy really stood out.*

Week 11: Too much of a good thing can be wonderful.

The aim for this week was to create a context in which the young women could celebrate some of their achievements. We began by asking:

- *What things are said and/or done to girls and young women that might encourage them to minimise or hide their achievements?*

We invited the young women to discuss the following questions in small groups:

- *How much of the time does the belief that it is not acceptable if you think you are good at something, stop you from recognising your achievements and believing people when they give you compliments?*
- *What has it stopped you from seeing about yourself and your achievements?*

After reflecting on these conversations back in the larger group, we then invited each participant to imagine what it would be like if they stood up to the belief that too much praise is a damaging thing. We asked the group to:

- *Imagine if you could recognise your own achievements, 'toot your own horn', and truly believe people when they gave you a compliment. What would be different about you and the way you feel about yourself?*

We asked the participants to represent on paper what would be different about them and the ways in which they feel about themselves, and to give this work a title. Some of the representations and titles included; 'Surprise', which was a drawing of a person with some of the qualities she had discovered written around the person; a drawing of a moving train that was moving past the station of disbelief; and 'I would', which listed some of the things this young woman would now do.

We ended the session on a round that we called 'tooting your own horn'. Each participant was given a party horn and was asked to toot their own horn by naming one thing that they really appreciated about themselves.

Week 12: Saying goodbye to the group and continuing on with the journey.

This was the last group session. We tried within this group to prepare people for the transition of leaving the group and continuing the journey of their lifetime. We invited the participants to get into pairs to discuss the question:

- *What are your fears about being without the group?*

Upon returning to the big group, we invited reflections about the small group discussions and asked the group to 'brainstorm' around the question:

- *What are you taking away from the group that will help you stand up to those fears?*

We then gave each participant a piece of paper with their name written on it. The other group members were asked to write down what their experience of travelling with this person during the last 12 weeks had been like and what they had appreciated about them. This was done for each person in the group.

To end the group we invited a final round orientated to the question:

- *What is something that the group has given you, that you would like the group to know you are taking with you on your journey?*

Some of the responses included: 'a greater sense of pride in myself'; 'knowing that I have a journey'; 'good memories'; 'my train's speeding up'; 'a shitometer that I will listen to'; 'the knowledge that I'm not insane'; 'feeling stronger in myself'; 'the strength to know I can continue on without the group'.

We gave out Passports and Tickets which represented that the preparation for the next part of the journey was complete. We also spent some time as facilitators thanking the young women and reflecting on what the group had meant to us (see below). As a thank you we gave the participants a small button that was the shape of a teapot on which we had drawn a golden heart. We wrapped this button up in a piece of paper on which was written a quote by Leela Anderson:

> *I was reminded of a small brooch a friend had made for me, a round and voluptuous silver tea-pot, with a golden heart in the middle of it. This gift symbolised a passing comment I had made about the meaning of connection in my life: how I thought all acts of revolution, perhaps particularly in women's lives, whether they be political or of the heart, began over a cup of tea. Somehow the birth of connection is, for me, in the ordinariness of acts like the sharing of tea.* (1995, p.24-25).

We talked about how this quote consistently reminds us of the importance of connection, and that it is out of the little things and the ordinary that the extraordinary comes. This also seemed very relevant as the sharing of food had been a significant part of the group. Then we partied!

Our experience of facilitating the group - dilemmas and reflections

Facilitating this group was truly an enriching experience that taught us much about working with young women, about facilitating groups, and about how we prefer to work with the people that come to our Service. There was great delight, much pain and sadness, many laughs, and a personal sense of fulfilment in watching how the group responded and participated in the group sessions. Each week we would all be inspired as the small, and large, ways in which these young women were reclaiming their lives emerged.

On reflection, one of the inspiring things for us as workers about the group was that it seemed to fit with how we wanted to be with the people who consult us. Right from the start there was a sense that this would also be a great journey for us as workers, and that we were also taking lots of risks and stepping into territory we hadn't been before. This led to us deciding to be very up-front, direct and honest with the group right from the beginning. We spent lots of time explaining why we were asking what we asked or what the thinking was behind a certain activity, and getting feedback on how it was going for the participants. This process contributed greatly to create an atmosphere of respect and trust that permeated the twelve weeks. The group members seemed to have a very real commitment to and respect for the group and each other. For us, as workers, the atmosphere of honesty and transparency gave us a freedom to relate as we wished to, rather than this be limited by how we thought 'professionals' should relate.

One of the most difficult aspects of facilitating the group was witnessing and giving space to hear some of the pain that was so present in these young women's lives. Many weeks we wondered if the participants were finding it too hard, if we were pushing them too far, and if they would keep travelling with us or get off at one of the points along the way. Checking with the group, and being really interested in how they were finding the sessions, was the only way to reassure ourselves that, although they were finding some of the sessions hard going, they were nonetheless very useful. There were many occasions when we had to stop ourselves from rushing in and trying to make things better which, in hindsight, were often times where we were feeling perhaps more uncomfortable than the group participants. Humour seemed to be as abundant as the pain, and was used so many times by the group as an antidote to diffuse some of the intensity. At times it seemed that the group members used humour to let us know also that it was okay to be talking about the things that we were.

Another theme that was present throughout many of the group sessions but which is not obvious when reading through the weekly outlines, was the young women's relationship with their mothers. This was often a difficult balancing act for us as facilitators as we wanted to expose some of the ways that mothers are often conned by the perpetrators of the abuse, whilst at the same time not excuse or minimise the pain that the young women felt as a result of some of the actions of their mothers. Often we were trying to bring the person who had committed the abuse back into the picture, as he had paled into insignificance against the rage some of the young women felt towards their mothers. For many of the young women the belief that they were unlovable, seemed to be cemented when they strongly held the idea that even their mother did not care about them, had not wanted to protect them, had not wanted to believe them, or loved the person who abused them more than they loved them. To challenge this belief it was essential to try and deconstruct some of the predominant ideas in society about mothers generally, and about mothers whose children have experienced sexual abuse. These issues were very significant in our discussions in week two about 'tricks, lies and bullshit'. Looking at how mothers are conned by perpetrators of child sexual abuse, and how men who abuse often try to shift responsibility to mothers, were important discussions to have.

At the same time, working with these young women brought many invitations from all kinds of discourses, and sometimes directly from the group members, to 'be their Mum' and to 'fix it all up'. Knowing the damage that creating this kind of expectation or hope can do, we were very up-front about the limits of what we could do. This, along with other aspects of the group, led us to re-think much of our training in what it means to be a professional, and what a professional relationship should be. Some of the most helpful learning for us was around the difference between having limits as a worker, or as a Service, as compared with the ideas of professional boundaries. In our experience, concepts of 'professional boundaries' had in the past left us feeling like we were not being true professionals if we disclosed information about ourselves, or if we showed our emotions whilst with someone with whom we were working, or if we connected with the people who consult with us not only as workers but as other women, other parents, etc. Challenging these ideas while maintaining a commitment to accountability and transparency was powerfully reclaiming of who we wanted to be as workers.

Being involved in this group was also inspiring in the amount of fun, creativity, and hope that it generated. Taking risks with how we structured the group, what conversations we had, what we revealed personally about ourselves: and then witnessing some of the results of those risks taken, was immensely sustaining. The 'journey of a lifetime' took us into territories we had not explored before. We look forward to the next one. Who knows where it will take us.

Acknowledgements

To the women who participated in the groups. Without their commitment, their skill and courage in taking many risks with us, and their immense patience, this group would never have happened.

To our colleagues at the Sexual Assault Support Service in Hobart for their support and encouragement for running a young women's group. In particular we would like to thank *Ruth Causon* for being able to transfer our vague ideas into documents with much flare and panache; *Jo Flanagan* for her ideas and assistance with the birth of the map; and *Clare Darling* for her enthusiasm and bravery in using these ideas in other groups - her suggestions, clarity, insights, and strong encouragement to actually write this up have been invaluable.

To *Jane Hutton*, for sharing her work and her pearls of creativity with us, and whose inspiration, courage, and vision have helped us to know that the journey was possible.

To *Amanda Kamsler* for providing us with an opportunity to talk about our experiences of facilitating this group, and for encouraging us to believe that these experiences were worthy of being shared with others.

Notes

1. First published in the 1998 Vol.1 *Gecko*. Republished here with permission.
2. Lisa and Chris were both counsellors at the Hobart Sexual Assault Support Service. They have since moved on. Chris can be contacted c/- Upper Murray CASA, PO Box 438, Wangaratta VIC 3676, Australia. Lisa can be contacted c/- 4 Creek St, Berridale NSW 2628, Australia.

   All group members gave permission to publish in this paper details of the group's experiences and their written work.

References

Anderson, L., 1995: 'Windows.' In Anderson, L. (ed), *Bedtime Stories For Tired Therapists*. Adelaide, South Australia: Dulwich Centre Publications.

Cora, D. & Linnell, S., 1993: *Discoveries: A Group Resource Guide for Women Who Have Been Sexually Abused in Childhood*. Sydney, NSW: Dympna House.

5

Questioning sexuality:
A workshop in progress[1]

by

Mark Trudinger, Cameron Boyd
& Peter Melrose[2]

The young men in our workshop on sexuality, masculinity, and homophobia, have just burst out laughing. On the television screen out front, Homer Simpson is worried that his son, Bart, will become gay, and has taken him to a steel mill to see 'all-American Joes'. But Homer freaks out when he realises that all the steelworkers in the mill are gay and, completely taken off-guard, yells out as if to insult them, 'You're all gay'. From the back of the foundry a blue singleted, muscly arm goes up, the hand bent over with a supposedly gay 'limp wrist' and, accompanied by the lisped, camp reply, 'Oh, be nice'.

Homophobic violence and honouring young queer men's strengths

It's good to be able to run a workshop on homophobia and have young men - and their male teacher - laughing at issues that often draw a deluge of homophobic comments, or a stony wall of silence - or both. The workshop we normally run in high schools, 'Step by step' (Denborough 1996), deals with issues of dominant constructions of masculinity and violence towards women, children, and - to an extent - gay and bisexual men. For a while we'd been wanting to develop a workshop specifically addressing issues of homophobia and sexuality, as we saw these issues as crucial to our anti-violence work with young men. The stories young men constantly tell us, our own experiences of high school, and literature about young people and sexuality, all showed us that homophobia plays a big part in the violence that young men experience - and engage in - at school.[2]

Daily experiences of harassment, violence, marginalisation, homelessness, drug use, and suicide, are common problems in the lives of young gay and bisexual men. Homophobia also impacts on the lives of all straight young men (and young men who don't identify sexually), as homophobia and homophobic violence are used as a form of surveillance to keep young men's (perceived) heterosexual masculinity in check. In running a workshop on these issues, we therefore hoped to create not only a more positive space for gay and bisexual young men, but for *all* young men.

We also hoped to find ways of honouring the strengths of young queer men and the resistances of young men to homophobia. This wish was informed by the young men who have come out to us after workshops; a local young gay man who came out and then set up a student-run resource room for *all* students at his school; and the experiences of one of the authors of this paper who identified as queer while at high school. In our general workshop, 'Step by step', to honour young queer men's strengths we usually ask what would happen if a student came out as gay, and the young men talk of the violence and harassment a queer student would face. We always follow this with questions such as: 'What would it say, then, about someone who could come to school every day and cop that?' or 'What strengths would it take to deal with that?' The young men's responses to these questions are often quite moving - they are suddenly talking of young queer men as 'strong', 'brave' and 'courageous'. We have also used this question in the following workshop on sexuality and homophobia.

Other resistances to homophobia

We also regularly see other significant resistances to homophobia from straight men in our general workshop (or young men who are *perceived* to be straight). Many of the instances the young men name as times they have stepped outside of dominant ideas of being a man also challenge culturally dominant ideas about heterosexuality, such as enjoying cooking, or having close relationships with their mothers, sisters, or another man. We are usually quick to ask questions that reflect on what it means for young men to do these things (again, see Denborough 1996).

There are some moments, however, where the profundity of what the young men talk about doesn't need any questions from us - times when young men's stories touch everyone in the room and act as a fantastic counterpoint to what 'real men should be like'. For example, in our general workshop, at least one young straight man usually speaks passionately about a friendship with another man. At a workshop we ran recently, one of the 'toughest-looking' young men spoke of his connection with his best friend, ending his story with, 'I love him, ey, he's my best mate. I love him, and I don't care what anyone says.' At this, the usually talkative group of young men fell completely silent! The importance of the moment also stopped us as facilitators in our tracks - one of us was trying not to start sobbing, and both of us didn't know what to say for a few minutes! (We were saved by a humorous but well-intentioned comment from one of the other young men, which broke the tension of the moment and reinforced the specialness of what the first young man said.) What did it say about one of the 'tough guys' that he could speak of his love for his mate? What opportunities and spaces might this have created for the other young men in the room?

An approach based on respect and hope

Our chance to develop a specific workshop exploring sexuality and homophobia came when a school accidentally booked us for a very large group of young men, and our normal small and intimate workshop would have had limited usefulness. So, *The Simpsons* episode in hand, we walked in, almost hoping the video would do the work for us. We hadn't planned much in the way of follow-up questions, and found ourselves in the tricky situation of having opened a space for the young men to talk about sexuality, only to face a barrage of homophobia. And, although we didn't use such words, we felt afterwards that we had then tried to show why the young men were 'wrong' or 'homophobic' ... not a very helpful or respectful orientation!

Time for a rethink ... We were keen to explore constructions of sexuality and homophobia from a more respectful approach to working with young people. We had used ideas drawn from deconstruction and narrative therapy, especially 'externalising conversations', in our previous work in schools about violence, and wondered how we could apply these approaches to talking about issues of sexuality and homophobic violence.[3] We were aware of the problems of simply externalising 'violence', or 'homophobic violence' (see Jenkins 1990), and decided to first discuss constructions of sexuality and then externalise aspects of homophobia and heterosexual masculinity - or what the young men often call 'being a man'.

We've only run the following workshop a couple of times, and it's still evolving, so what's written here are really just beginning notes. We'd appreciate any comments or suggestions for additions that readers may have. What we *have* found so far is that, unlike the 'anything goes' general discussion we attempted, this workshop has given us immense amounts of hope - about a topic, and in a context, where it can sometimes be difficult to find invitations of hope.[4]

Part 1: What's the difference?

The episode of *The Simpsons* we show the young men has many reflections of dominant - and subversive - ideas of heterosexuality and homosexuality (Hauge 1997). These provide us with useful discussion points of the interweavings of sexuality and masculinity. To begin with, we draw two columns on the board and ask the young men what the differences are between how straight and gay men are portrayed in the episode.

We then write up these differences the young men noticed, and other areas we may have noticed. For example, to get the process rolling we may ask: 'What about bodies? How did straight men's bodies look? What about the gay men's?' or, 'How did the different men respond to anger, or in difficult situations?'[5] At the end of this process we end up with a list something like in the box below.

	Straight	Gay
Bodies	fat and unfit	skinny, or very muscly
Pastimes	drinking	kitsch antique collecting
Responding to difficult situations	anger	humour
Dancing	an oddity	a part of life
Relating to women	patronising, accusing	conversational
Relating to children	controlling	respects them, takes them places

During the process of making this list, we are very careful to say that this is 'how the men were portrayed in the video', and link this to dominant ideas of masculinity and sexuality. This does two useful things. First, the video provides a quick sketch of the supposed differences between heterosexual and homosexual men, and provides more immediate material than trying to have us and the young men come up with examples from everyday life which, as we had discovered, can sometimes be slow going for topics as touchy as sexuality and homophobia.

Second, it sets a context for externalising dominant constructions of heterosexual masculinity and homosexual masculinity: talking about 'how the men were portrayed in the video' and linking this to 'dominant ideas about men and sexuality', helps lay a linguistic framework that situates ideas about men and sexuality 'out there', as part of the dominant culture, not as aberrant notions held by young men who 'need to be changed'. We've found that this general framework, and the specific externalising questions that come later, go some ways to side-stepping the previously 'inevitable' wave of homophobic comments that would appear when we simply had an unstructured conversation, or said 'let's talk about homosexuality'. This very different way of having a conversation, in turn, allows for a different role for us as facilitators. It allows us to join with the young men to co-investigate and, in the rest of the workshop, to 'co-expose' dominant ideas around masculinity and sexuality, rather than acting as 'the anti-homophobia police' that we sometimes felt like in previous workshops.

We're not talking stereotypes

An important distinction in language - and therefore practice - in our approach is that we try to avoid using the word 'stereotypes'. We know that this concept initially provided a useful starting point for reflecting on cultural practices. However, we've also come to think it has some limitations. For example, when I (MT) went to high school in the late 1980s, teachers used the word 'stereotypes' so often that it almost became meaningless. Or, more accurately, stereotypes were 'straw people' or concepts that *didn't exist in reality*, so, as young people, we dismissed not only the 'stereotype' under discussion, but the *whole stereotype framework/analysis that went with it*, so well-intentioned lessons weren't as effective as they could have been.

It's only been after running these workshops that I think I understand why we as students did this: the idea of stereotypes presents concepts that can simply be shown to be 'not true', and then dismissed. What it usually doesn't do is show the meaning-making aspects of culture - of how dominant ideas inform people's lives, and also how these meanings are contested, negotiated, and subverted. Stereotype frameworks also don't often provide ways to move forward, or open a space for other ways of being to be honoured: once you've exposed something as a 'stereotype', what's next? It also seems disrespectful and counterproductive to discuss aspects of young men's lives and then label these stereotypic.

While we are careful not to use the word 'stereotype' in our workshops, sometimes a young man will. When young men in our workshops point to a list such as the one above and say, 'But that's just stereotypes', it's important for us to talk about how, while these ideas may not ever be fully adhered to in real life, they still are an important influence on how we are as men. But, rather than get too caught up in this line of conversation, we usually ask the young man more useful questions about why he pointed it out. What we've found is that, when young men have said 'they're just stereotypes', they have been not just critiquing a stereotype model, but also *protesting* the dominant prescriptions of masculinity. They have gone on to say that such a list is unrealistic, unfair, or to point out contradictions to the list from the video itself, or their own lives. When this happens, as it often does, this provides a wonderful lead-in to the next part of the workshop.

Part 2: Questioning the differences

When the above list of binary oppositions is up on the board, we're keen to quickly put some context around it - to deconstruct it, rather than let it reinforce problematic ideas. We use the following questions to explore the list of binaries, and for the reasons that follow:

1. *What messages does this list give us about the supposed differences between gay and straight men?*

2. *What might be some consequences of these messages - to gay men, to straight men, to women, and to the other characters in the video?*

3. *Are these differences real / do they exist in real life?*

4. *What are some of the exceptions / contradictions you know of? What about examples in the video, other movies, from your lives, or from other men you know?*

5. *With the consequences you mentioned, and the contradictions you pointed out, why, then, might some men try to make clearly-defined differences between gay and straight men?*

Question one: Right from the beginning we are keen to speak in ways that lessen the chance of young men engaging in homophobic language, and instead *exposing* how sexuality and homophobia are constructed. Talking about the 'messages the list gives us', or the 'messages that the ways the men are shown in the video', helps externalise these practices from the outset.

Question two: Sometimes answers to this question are slow in appearing, so we follow it up with specific examples from the video and from the list the young men come up with. So we might ask: 'What are the consequences to men to drink constantly?' or, 'What are the consequences on other characters of Homer wanting to make sure that Bart isn't gay?' These questions usually expose some of the costs of a dominating heterosexual masculinity - costs to gay men, straight men, young men, and the other people in straight men's lives.

Question three: We do not ask this question to search for 'truth', but to open a space for the young men's contradictions and contestations to this list, asked about in the next question. This question has also allowed for the young men to say that this list is 'not real but sort of expected', which further helps to externalise dominant concepts of sexuality.

Question four: By this stage the young men we've worked with are usually *very* keen to point out contradictions. The list of 'straight' attributes, which many of them would normally expect to align themselves with, aren't usually things they aspire to. Of course they are quick to point out that *The Simpsons* is satire, or that the list is simply 'stereotypical', but they also know that this list does contain many of the expected scripts and behaviours of dominant heterosexual masculinity. This, then, provides space for a broader investigation of these ideas and, in the workshops we have run so far, has led to the young men both rejecting dominant ideas of masculinity, redeeming attributes that might be considered 'sissy' or 'gay', and then questioning such distinctions between heterosexuality and homosexuality. Again, this is a far more subtle and complex conversation than just one about 'stereotypes'. This question also often leads young men to protest about systems of power and meaning that they have had relatively little say in forming, and do not fit for them - they say that they didn't ask for things to be the way they are. While this is an important issue, we are also keen to provide a context later in the workshop that allows for the privileges and benefits of heterosexuality to also be named.

Question five: This question is not to downplay the importance of actual differences between straight and gay men which, in our theoretical orientation and practice, we regard as important and something that can be both a site of celebration and sharing. Rather, we ask this question to explore the *perceived* differences, usually ones perpetrated by heterosexual masculinity, in a context of discriminating against gay men. Ideally, this question will lead to a young man in the group naming homophobia, and then into the next part of the workshop. At times this question has seemed useful to lead us to homophobia as a discussion point - at other times it has seemed a little obscure. We'll probably come up with another question more concrete in language and reliable in taking the group to a discussion about homophobia.

Part 3: Questioning homophobia

Homophobia usually is named in the previous section, so we move on to what we call 'questioning', or deconstructing, homophobia. We decided to work specifically with homophobia and not heterosexual dominance generally, because in some ways it seems more concrete and more immediately relevant to boys and schoolyard culture, and because it is more easily linked to issues of violence. Also, we've found that most schools have named homophobia in other contexts such as human relationships education, or lessons on discrimination. This means that we can ask for some definitions of homophobia, and be fairly sure that some will be offered. (An important note: We don't ask for just 'a' or 'the' definition - we don't want to create an environment where there are right or wrong answers that we have to evaluate, and we *do* want to create an environment where many voices can be heard.)

Again, the following questions have been created to externalise homophobia, or to talk about it in a way that locates it as part of the general culture, and not within the young men we work with. In asking the questions, we begin by referring to the men in the video the young men just saw so that issues aren't too 'close to home'. We move on to ask for other examples the young men can think of as the questions progress:

1. *What does homophobia have to say about how straight men should relate to each other? To men they think are gay?*

2. *What does homophobia say about how men should relate to children?*

3. *What are some of the costs of homophobia to men - to gay men, to straight men, to young men?*

4. *What are some of the costs of men's homophobia to women?* (The video provides an excellent example of mother-blame when Homer blames Marge for Bart being gay. The young men we work with often have many other examples of homophobia and mother-blame working together.)

5. *What are some of the benefits to straight men?*

Part 4: Questioning heterosexual masculinity

The final question in the previous section leads us neatly to questioning heterosexual masculinity which, for simplicity's sake, and to show the link between heterosexuality and dominant constructions of masculinity, we refer to in our workshops as 'being a man'. This workshop usually follows a previous workshop where the young men give their own name to the 'dominant plot' of masculinity. If we remember, we use their words here to show the same link. Here are the questions we've asked and some quick background and reflections:

1. *What do dominant ideas about 'being a man' say about how men should relate to nature in the video?*

2. *What do dominant ideas about 'being a man' say about men and health, about how men should treat their bodies?*

3. *When Homer is worried that Bart may not be straight, he sits him down in front of a billboard with two bikini-clad women. How do dominant ideas of being a man have men treating women?*

4. *When Homer finds out that John is gay, he doesn't want to have anything to do with him and loudly protests his own heterosexuality. What are some of the ways that ideas about 'being a man' have men policing, or keeping an eye on, themselves and others?*

5. *What are some of the exceptions to 'being a man' that straight men did in the video?*

Question one: The question about nature really gets young men talking. It refers to a key part of the episode when Homer takes Bart out to kill a deer to make sure he's a 'real' (read heterosexual) man. We found this to be a disturbing, but not too unrealistic, portrayal of the scarier aspects of heterosexual masculinity with its equations of sex as 'on the prowl / hunt', and nature equated with women, and both to be controlled, used, or killed, as men see fit. The young men also pick up on these equations and also seem concerned by them. Some have told us of similar incidents that have happened in their lives.

Question two: It's good to have concrete examples to use in discussing health issues. In *The Simpsons*, generally, Homer drinks a lot of beer. In the episode we show, after an embarrassing encounter with some reindeer, Mo, the bartender, says, 'Well, it's suicide for me again'. The irony of this joke gives way to a useful discussion of the relationship between success / failure, and men's physical and mental health. Questions such as: 'Why might Mo say such a thing? What's the relationship between perceived failure and who we are as men?' have led to interesting discussions in a relatively non-threatening way.

Question three: As one young man pointed out, in the video Homer didn't even see the billboard as an advertisement for a product, he sees near-naked women. This leads to a discussion about objectification, and the young men name current billboards that use women's bodies to sell products.

Question four: Our own memories of high school, and comments from young men we work with, show that young men are under almost constant 'heterosexuality surveillance' - either by other young men or self-surveillance. This can affect most aspects of young men's lives, from how they spend time with other men, how they relate to women, and even how they hold their own bodies.

Question five: Again, talking about the exceptions is crucial in creating a space for alternative ways of being for men. From here, the workshop has led to discussions of alternatives in the young men's own lives, and we're quick to ask them their reflections on what these exceptions mean.

Next steps ...

We're keen to run this workshop with more young men and find more questions that lead to useful discussion. We're not sure just how we'll do it yet, but we're curious to find ways to have conversations which explore the implications of bisexuality and postmodern ideas about sexuality in creating new language and understand of power, desire and identity. We also hope to work more in the coming year with women who are working with young women around issues of violence, gender, and homophobia. Having realised that most young queer men cannot speak about their sexuality while at school, we're also keen to explore the possibility of inviting young queer men who've recently left school to talk with the young men we work with. We're both cautious and excited about what might happen in such conversations. While this work has been, and will continue to be, at times tricky and fraught, we're always inspired by what the young men have to say - their everyday examples that offer each other as young men, and us as older men, immense amounts of hope that men can find less violent, more caring ways of being.

Thanks

Thanks to the people who've informed and supported the work we do in schools: *Darlene Corry, Mark D'Astoli, David Denborough, Chris Krogh, Chris McLean, Martin Mills, David Newman, Maria Pallotta-Chiarolli, and Jacinta Toomey.*

Notes

1. First published in the 1998 No.4 *Dulwich Centre Journal*. Republished here with permission.
2. Mark, Cameron & Peter can be contacted c/- Young Men's Anti-Violence Project, PO Box 5375, West End QLD 4101, Australia, phone (61-7) 3399 4181.
3. For some of the issues that queer young peoples face, see DeCrescenzo (1994), Harbeck (1992), Heron (1994), Laskey & Beavis (1996) and Beckett (1998).
4. For more on externalising problems, see White & Epston (1990) and White (1998). For other work in schools using externalising exercises, see 'Taking the hassle out of school and stories from younger people', *Dulwich Centre Journal*, 1998 Nos.2&3, and 'Schooling and education: Exploring new possibilities', *Dulwich Centre Newsletter*, 1995 Nos.2&3.
5. 'Step by step' (Denborough 1996) contains important considerations of power and group process that we also follow in this workshop.
6. This question refers to how the male characters chose to respond to difficult situations. In the video, Homer responds with anger, aggression, insults, and by attempting to control others, while the gay men use humour such as in the steel mill example that opened this piece. Because our work has come from wanting to reduce men's violence, clear examples of the choices available to men that show that violence is not inevitable or biological, are very useful.

References

Beckett, L. (ed) 1998: *Everyone is Special! A handbook for teachers on sexuality education*. Sandgate, Queensland: Association of Women Educaters.

DeCrescenzo, T. (ed) 1994: *Helping Gay and Lesbian Youth: New policies, new programs, new practice*. New York: Harrington Park Press.

Denborough, D. 1996: 'Step by step: Developing respectful and effective ways of working with young men to reduce violence.' In McLean, C., Carey, M. & White, C. (eds), *Men's Ways of Being*. Boulder, Co: Westview Press.

Harbeck, K.M. (ed) 1992: *Coming Out in the Classroom Closet: Gay and lesbian students, teachers, and curricula*. New York: Harrington Park Press.

Hauge, R. 1997: 'Homer Phobia.' An episode of *The Simpsons*. Original airdate was 16th February 1997, on Fox Television.

Heron, A. 1994: *Two Teenagers in Twenty: Writings by gay and lesbian youth*. Boston: Alyson Publications.

Jenkins, A. 1990: *Invitations to Responsibility: The therapeutic engagement of men who are violent and abusive*. Adelaide: Dulwich Centre Publications.

Laskey, L. & Beavis, C. 1996: *Schooling and Sexualities: Teaching for a positive sexuality*. Geelong, Victoria: Deakin Centre for Education and Change.

'Schooling and education: Exploring new possibilities.' *Dulwich Centre Newsletter*, 1995 Nos.2&3.

'Taking the hassle out of school and stories from younger people.' *Dulwich Centre Journal*, 1998 Nos.2&3.

White, M. 1998: 'Notes on externalising problems.' In White, C. & Denborough, D. (eds), *Introducing Narrative Therapy: A collection of practice-based writings*. Adelaide: Dulwich Centre Publications.

White, M. & Epston, D. 1990: *Narrative Means to Therapeutic Ends*. New York: W.W.Norton.

PART III

Community
Work

6

Communities
of shared experience[1]

from an interview with

Maggie Carey[2]

Here in Australia and elsewhere, current economic and political discourses are resulting in cuts to the funding of programs provided to those who are unable to pay for counselling services. This is resulting in heartfelt dilemmas for many service providers. Continuing pressure is being applied to workers to 'make the most' of available resources while juggling the impact of ever-increasing waiting lists and having to work with the uncertainty as to whether programs will continue.

The work described in this paper is one of the responses of the Adelaide Central Mission, South Australia (a large non-government organisation based in the inner-city of Adelaide), to this situation. It explores an alternative to traditional office-based counselling - an alternative that involves the collaboration of workers across various agencies in facilitating gatherings of people who are struggling to overcome similar problems in their lives. This paper has been written in the hope of inspiring others to respond to the current economic and political environment with increased creativity.

Working with violence and abuse

For many years at the counselling service of the Adelaide Central Mission we've been working with families who have been struggling with the effects of violence and abuse. As counsellors we are often privileged within conversations to witness members of these families making significant changes to the ways in which they understand their lives. We are often privileged to witness people feeling more in charge of the problems that concern them. And yet, when these people return to contexts which so powerfully support the problems in their lives, we are often left wondering how these changes will be sustained.

It has become increasingly clear how large a part isolation plays in maintaining the effects of violence and abuse. Often there isn't anybody else in these people's lives outside of the counselling sessions to witness the preferred understandings by which they are wanting to live their lives and the steps that they have been taking. The lack of other outsider-witnesses in these people's lives can be a powerful restraint in freeing themselves from the effects of violence and abuse. It also means that we as counsellors play the role of witnessing and authenticating changes. Recently we have begun to wonder whether we are the best people to be doing this work.

In response to this situation we have decided that we need to find some other ways of working that create a context in which the changes people are making to their lives can be magnified, anchored and experienced much more solidly. We are particularly interested in finding ways in which families who have similar experiences can share their learnings, knowledges and skills. Within counselling sessions, when we share with particular people what other people have done in similar situations, we often witness that this facilitates the possibility for people to break from a sense of 'there's something wrong with me'. We wish to take this further. Over the last eighteen months we have explored ways of working that more directly contribute to the building of communities of shared experience.

As a first step we decided that we would hold a gathering for women and their children who had experienced violence in their homes. [3]

Gatherings of women and children

The first gathering we held was with mothers and children who had been affected by violence and abuse. There were twenty-seven children aged from two to seventeen; nineteen women; eight counsellors from four different agencies; and two child-care workers! The child care workers were to care for the children under the age of five. A group of counsellors, of which I was a part, were to work with the older children. The gathering was held over three days at a rural setting south of Adelaide.

We plan to write up the experience of this gathering so I will not focus on the content here in any detail. There were, however, many significant events. Early on we held externalising conversations in which one of the male counsellors (who has considerable experience working with men who are violent) played the role of Mr Power & Control and Mr Mother-Blame. The women delighted in asking many questions of him, exposing both his tactics and his weaknesses.[4] We held sessions in which the women explored the effects of the violence and the ways in which they stood against these effects both in their own lives and the lives of their children. Listening groups witnessed these stories, and rituals of acknowledgement took place. There were consistent conversations about the ongoing effects of violence on the women's relationships with their children. With this broader context acknowledged, conversations about the replication of violence - from mother to child, between children, and from children to mothers, also occurred. The effects of this violence were discussed, as were the ways in which the women and children were trying to address it.

We'd spent a lot of time planning the conversations with the women and much less time thinking through how we would work with the children. Throughout the gathering we were busily finding ways to have conversations with the children in all sorts of different contexts - from cycling through paddocks occupied by bulls, to canoeing in a treacherous dam, to tumbling down hills while worrying about snakes! It was an incredibly active couple of days. We now refer to it as 'therapy on the run'. We found that we could have really excellent and challenging conversations in these sorts of contexts.

At this first gathering a number of lesbian mothers who had left heterosexual relationships in which there had been violence were clear that they wanted and needed a separate context in which to discuss the effects of homophobia and heterosexual dominance on their relationships with their children. This core group of lesbian women became our consultants to set up a further gathering which we held for lesbian mothers and their children.

Since then we have also held another gathering for heterosexual women and their children and we have a number of further gatherings planned. One is to be for young mothers with children five years old and younger who have been affected by violence and abuse. This will be focussed on re-storying the relationship between the kids and their mums. We are also interested in a gathering of gay men who are parents, and a gathering for homeless men who wish to address issues of violence.

What seems to work

In all of the gatherings so far there have been a number of things that I have found particularly energising. The ways in which violence affects women's relationship with their children is a very private issue and one that is easily stigmatised. Normalising this situation appears to be very important. Being with others who are experiencing the same sorts of questions, fears and problems acts as an antidote to stigma. Creating a situation in which women and children know that the others present have had similar experiences seems to enable them to more easily separate from ideas of self-blame. The gatherings seem to provide a powerful audience to the fact that the violence did not occur due to some flaw in themselves. Being in it together seems to enable the women and children to much more quickly get in touch with their own skills and knowledges because they are quick to recognise them in the others around them. All of this seems to reduce a sense of isolation and generate hopefulness.

What I particularly enjoy is the way in which a gathering can enable very different relationships between counsellors and the women and children. When we're all eating together; washing up together; waking up in the same environment, there are so many opportunities for different conversations and different sorts of sharing. What we as counsellors bring to the work, the rest of our lives, is much more apparent. Similarly, we get to know so much more about other aspects of the women's lives and the children's lives. We get to know aspects of their lives that have nothing to do with the problems that they are dealing with. In counselling sessions a lot of time is spent talking about the problem, or people's relationship to the problem, or the ways in which people are overcoming a problem. When together at a gathering whole other landscapes of life become more visible.

In some way this appears to normalise therapeutic conversations. When living together in a community, if only for a few days, the 'therapeutic conversations' become part of an every-day living. Of course there are particular structured conversations within the gathering as well, but lots of the important conversations occur over dinner, or breakfast, or on the way to the showers. Enabling conversations cease being things that happen only in the therapist's office and become things that happen in all areas of life. In working with the children in particular, these informal conversations seem to offer far greater possibilities than talking in an office. In fact, while on the gathering, the idea of talking in an office seemed a bit crazy!

Working as part of a listening group is also something I really enjoy. After the first gathering all the counsellors spoke of how generative it was to be able to build upon each other's contributions and develop a real sense of teamwork. For me it is an energising way of working.

Different experiences

What is particularly helpful about the gatherings, I think, is that they create a context in which the women and children (and the counsellors for that matter) can experience themselves differently, and where family members can experience other family members differently. Many women made comments like, 'I had never seen that side of my daughter or my son ...' or, 'I'd never actually seen that they could, you know, be like that'. In this way the gatherings opened up a whole lot of possibilities for people to experience themselves and each other differently, and conversations about the meaning of these experiences could then take place. This was so important because the main issue we wanted to address was the relationship between the mothers and their children.

In some gatherings we didn't have any sessions with mothers and children together - but we consistently fed back to the women what was happening in our times with the children. We discussed the issues that the children were raising and what we were talking about. The women really enjoyed hearing about these conversations. On the gathering with lesbian mothers the children wrote and performed a song of appreciation back to their mothers. The song also spoke of the effects of homophobia. There wasn't a dry eye in the audience. These sorts of shared experiences on the gatherings can offer a sense of connection and sustenance. Their effects last far longer than the gathering itself.

Ongoing connections

The setting of a gathering also enables different sorts of connections to form. For example, one nine-year-old boy was able to say to his mum after the gathering, 'I think I need to talk to someone, and I want it to be Fiona'. Fiona was a particular worker who he had spent time with. In this way the gathering enabled a counselling relationship to be established from a context of real choice for the child. Support groups for the children have also evolved from the gatherings, as well as close friendships. At the end of each gathering many of the children swap phone numbers. For both the women and the children, connections made at the gatherings can provide an ongoing witness to the changes they are making in their lives and the skills and knowledges that these changes represent.

Quite apart from all the other advantages, the gatherings are also a very efficient use of resources. Over the three days there are so many opportunities for conversations: breakfast, lunch and dinner, morning and afternoon tea, and then right into the evening. And this is quite apart from the structured exercises and conversations! There are so many hours of contact over a short time. We have tried to estimate the value of the gatherings and worked out that each of the counsellors did the equivalent of five weeks of one-to-one counselling over the three days! But you can't compare the conversations on the gatherings to one-to-one work because at the gatherings we have available the invaluable resource of a collective pool of understanding, knowledges and skills. This makes every interaction magnified in some way. When looking at any issue there is so much to draw upon. What's more, there are constant rituals of acknowledgement from people who have experienced similar things, as well as from the listening teams. There is an audience that is not available in one-to-one work. Importantly, these experiences themselves then become available to be called upon in future one-to-one conversations. They become reference points. Questions can be asked like, 'When you were experiencing yourself in that way what was that about?' People can be invited to get in touch with their experiences of the gathering at later times. A solid experience of alternative ways of relating becomes forever available.

The future

I am hoping that we will facilitate gatherings every month or so. In this way the experience of different ways of relating could become more regularly available. I'd like to see that building communities of shared experience becomes a significant aspect of our work, and that gatherings become a regular adjunct to counselling. For me, working in these ways is an opportunity to involve so many more aspects of myself in the work. It is a joy to me to be having significant conversations while tumbling down hills or riding a bike! I find that I draw on other aspects of my self and my life in the relationships that are formed on these gatherings. I'd like to explore the possibilities further.

Counsellors who have been involved in one or more of the gatherings discussed in this paper:

Maggie Carey, Adelaide Central Mission

Leslye Chenery, Nunkuwarrin Yunti Aboriginal Health Service

Molly Claire, Women's Health Statewide

Jussey Harbord, Salisbury West Community Health Service

Ian Law, Adelaide Central Mission

Iain Lupton, Adelaide Central Mission

Mahamati, Adelaide Central Mission, Bfriend Project

Carolyn Markey, Centacare

Sue McKinnon, Northern Metropolitan Community Health Service

Lise Moodle, Shopfront
Aerrin Morgan, Mental Health Services
Anne Morris, Northern Women's Community Health Service
Patrick O'Leary, Adelaide Central Mission
Brod Osbourne, Adelaide Central Mission
Pam Price, Women's Health Statewide
Shona Russell, Adelaide Central Mission
Tracey Sloan, Adelaide Central Mission
Margaret Wild, Women's Health Statewide

Notes

1. This paper evolved from an interview with David Denborough. It was first published in the 1998 Vol.1 *Gecko*. Republished here with permission.
2. Maggie can be contacted c/- Adelaide Central Mission, 10 Pitt Street, Adelaide 5000, South Australia.
3. For an acknowledgement of the history of ideas that has led us to explore gatherings as a means of honouring shared experience and finding appropriate ways of healing, see: 'Reclaiming Our Stories, Reclaiming Our Lives' (1995), *Dulwich Centre Newsletter* No.1 (special issue), and 'Speaking Out and Being Heard' (1995), *Dulwich Centre Newsletter* No.4 (special issue).
4. White, M. 1999: 'Notes on externalising problems.' In White, C. & Denborough, D. (eds), *Introducing Narrative Therapy: A collection of practice-based writings.* Adelaide: Dulwich Centre Publications.

7

Strengthening communities and promoting health[1]

by

Pat-Ann[2]

Inner Southern Community Health Service (ISCHS), the oldest community health centre in South Australia, was established in the mid-1970s. It has a long tradition of working in partnership with local community activists. This is the story of a community development initiative which began in February 1997 and has grown in ways that have surprised and delighted the participants and the worker.

In 1996 the ISCHS had run a successful, skills-based education program for community activists focussed on group dynamics, motivation and lobbying techniques. However, during and between group sessions, other themes were emerging. Participants were saying that, after what seemed like years of struggle in community work, they were feeling under pressure, stressed and unsupported in their actions. The major themes of these conversations reflected exhaustion, frustration, and disillusionment, but also the occasional 'win' against the odds, cruelly adding to the pressure on them to keep going at any cost. It became clear they were asking for time out to replenish and nourish themselves, and to rethink their ideas about what it meant to be an activist.

In response to these conversations, ISCHS gave a commitment for a worker to be involved with a new group whose aim would be to promote the health and well-being of unpaid community activists. Worker support was provided throughout 1997. The group, with its original seven participants, has subsequently continued to meet without the worker.

The group began with seven local people involved, each of whom had a herstory/history of community activism spanning many years. They were involved in issues related to the environment, Vietnam veterans, disabilities and education, community consultative groups, mental health issues, and the setting up of support groups for people dealing with various government agencies.

At the first gathering it was clarified that this was not a group that would ask activists to 'do more'. Instead, an invitation was extended to name what gave them joy and nourishment in their work and to explore what meaning social activism held for them:

Our initial goal was to strengthen ourselves and each other.

When it was suggested no-one would need to 'do anything' and there would be no push to develop any particular action together, several people cried. It was a powerful and surprising response to being invited to 'not do anything' but to simply spend the time with each other in reflection and analysis, discovering what their activism has meant to them and their communities. They explained the tears came from the exhaustion they were experiencing. This exhaustion, they said, was part of the ongoing personal cost of social activism in the 1990s. The commitment to each other which was forged in those early meetings was based on their mutual understanding of the effort required and the costs incurred by being willing to stand up for their beliefs and their respective communities:

People often start a support group as a result of an injustice. It is a difficult path ... a big responsibility ... there's intimidation, rejection ... the process can damage people.

At one of the initial gatherings it was decided to use a newsletter format to record the ideas and insights that emerged as the group evolved. The newsletters became an extension of the group process as each person added their thoughts, cartoons were used, and quotations of particular interest were included. Most people missed very few meetings and so the newsletter was much more to them than an update of information. It played the role of expanding the threads of the conversations held in the meetings. The newsletter continues to be produced monthly by different members of the group. One participant commented:

I love the newsletters - they go up on the fridge with my daughter's paintings - they make me smile and they make me think.

As the group began the process of exploring their activism, and its impact on their lives as well as the community at large, they drew ideas from narrative ways of working, theories of social construction, and critical analysis. The works of John Ralston Saul, Eva Cox, Noam Chomsky, Matthew Fox, Michael White, and Simone Weil were used to assist in the dissection of the ways dominant cultures overcome criticism and encourage compliant citizenship. People exchanged stories of different strategies that were used against them to keep them quiet or to undermine their attempts to have their questions answered. Many had experienced the politics of dividing activists, pitting one group against another, and the bitterness that caused in previously close-knit communities:

I need the bonding, strength, support and education I get from the ... group.

The power of language was examined and an analysis undertaken of how language can be used to exclude people who disagree with the 'owners' of the language. One of the participants brought a letter she had received from a government agency which had requested her presence as a community representative at a consultation on local issues. When she had asked to be paid for her consultation in the same manner as others on the consultative group, she was gently and politely refused payment. With much laughter and fun the letter was dissected into the 'standing with' language and the 'unfortunately standing against' language. The point of the analysis was not to blame the agency for its letter, but to better understand how and when language is being used for or against people, and lay bare the concept that language is allegedly neutral:

They told me professional people were paid to be on this consultative group but not community reps. Were they saying that community reps were of less importance?

The group also began to identify some of the strategies of disenfranchising people that they had encountered, including dividing communities against each other, name-calling, and even intimidation. Placing these stories within a greater sociopolitical context allowed for an extensive exploration of what strategies are used in an attempt to silence and push activists back into a more compliant stance. Standing back from the invitation to be immobilised by these tactics created a space for reflection and further assessment of how to deal with them. People told stories of how they had been compromised in their respective communities by agencies and companies using tactics of division. Implications of misbehaviour and possible criminal action were made, as well as allegations of wasting taxpayers' money. Suggestions were made that activists had their own interests at heart and were not actually representing the community at all:

I used to defend myself when they said I was just a trouble-maker ... now I quite like the name ... it was just an attempt to frighten me.

Much fun was had brainstorming a vast range of 'name-calling and labelling' that the members of the group had endured. Standing aside from these 'belittling' names and seeing the strategies behind the labelling had a powerful and profound effect on many people in the group. People had been called, at different times: communists, trouble-makers, selfish, uncaring, crazy, misguided, sole parents, bitter and twisted, feminists, and public nuisances. Another had been dismissed because of a mental health disability. There were many tears and much laughter as it became clear how common and interchangeable the list of 'belittling' names was, and how these names were attributed.

The very real effects of this name-calling and labelling were also discussed, and the ways in which it generated fear and made people fearful for themselves and their families were talked about at length. The negative impact on their emotional and physical health of these tactics of intimidation became more visible to group participants:

Marking the anniversary of survival

By the time the one year anniversary of the rape was coming up I felt I had to do something to mark the occasion. To say, 'Look, I'm still here. I haven't forgotten about it and it's just not going to go away. But I have survived.' The dominant way of viewing rape is to see the woman as a victim who feels ashamed and that she's got to forget about the rape, to get over the story of humiliation and shame, to bury it, to get back to normal. Whereas, if you believe in telling a story of survival then it's always progressing and ongoing. You're not going to forget but you're going to be moving along.

So on the anniversary of the rape I asked my friends out to dinner. When I first suggested this, I was nervous and I think the way that I invited people confused them a bit. I kind of announced it by saying, 'You know, the 15th of January that's my one year anniversary, I thought we could go out to dinner to celebrate'. And my friends thought what?! Celebrate that you got raped!? And then I could explain, 'No, to celebrate that I've survived'. I don't think we're used to talking about survival and so it can be confusing at times. Pretty quickly they understood that to stay at home on that night and watch videos would have been conforming to the victim role. It would have been staying inside away from the street, mourning what happened rather than going outside, being a part of life and saying, 'I'm still here'.

So we went out to dinner together. After we'd eaten, Nathan read out a speech which talked about the importance of friendship. He spoke of my courage too but mostly we wanted to stress how friendship had so helped the process of survival. One of the guys there then said that he thought I was one of the strongest women that he knew and how all of this had changed his attitudes to a lot of things. He spoke about how any tolerance he had once had for sexist jokes and all that kind of stuff had now completely gone. He said once he may have half-laughed and just let it go, but now he won't stand for it. He won't tolerate it at all. I was really glad that he could say that.

Another friend, who didn't come to the march, said something really helpful. I had been going on about how Davo had got away with it and she said that she hadn't spent any time thinking about Davo, that she didn't see the point. She said, 'I haven't thought about him at all because that's not important to me. It's you that's important to me. How you're coping. He doesn't deserve any of our attention in any way.'

It helped a lot. It made me think about one of the women in my counselling group. When the guy who raped her was being sentenced we stood outside the court and she just read her poetry - poems of her survival. There was a group of people, and the media was there. She was determined to take the attention away from the perpetrator. There's always so much attention on him. She wanted to focus some attention on the survivors and the stories of survival. That felt really good.

Another one of my friends, Fiona, who is really quiet and didn't say anything at the dinner, came up to me later. She said, 'I'm not religious, but I've been praying for you and thinking about you'. Fiona never says very much, she keeps to herself. When she does say something it's worth listening to.

Paul, another friend, came up to me some time later and apologised for not being more of a support. He said, 'I'm sorry but I've had a rough year myself. I just told my parents I was gay so I've been kind of dealing with that.'

Somehow we have all built up the trust between us. They are very special friendships to me. We have shared such rich histories. They are so much a part of my story of survival.

Sharing this story

Telling this story here, having it published, is like offering it to other people - hoping it might help. I think it is so important to share stories of survival.

Notes

1. First published in the 1998 Nos.2&3 *Dulwich Centre Journal*. Republished here with permission.
2. Cecily can be contacted c/- Dulwich Centre Publications, Hutt St PO Box 7192, Adelaide 5000, South Australia.

10

The story of temper[1]

by

Jai Wilson & Tracy Castelino[2]

Temper was having
a really good morning

Jai was, on the other hand,
having a really bad morning
so far

Temper had been at Jai
to kick Muffy the dog

who was now really sad

to pull the buds off
the beautiful new camellia plant

now the plant looked unhappy
and Mummy was upset

Temper even got Jai to grab
the apple off Daddy

Jai scratched Daddy and now
Daddy's arm was hurting

Daddy was sad

Now Jai was sad and upset too

Jai and Mummy had a talk about Temper and the trouble it caused for Jai and Mummy and Muffy and Daddy, and even the camellia plant!!

They talked about things they could do to get rid of Temper as it seemed to be causing lots of trouble for everybody

and they wondered what Jai could do to be the BOSS of Temper

Being the boss of Temper gave Jai a big smile

What could he do? He wondered what he could do

Maybe catch Temper and throw it to the sky

Really, really high

way up to the top of the sky

Or maybe Jai could put Temper in the back garden behind the tomato plants

Which idea would be good to try?

Jai was still feeling a little bit sad, but kept wondering at these new ideas while Mummy went into her office.

'Mummy?' called Jai. Mummy was doing some work in her office.

'Yes Jai,' Mummy called, 'I'm just putting these papers away'.

'Look at Temper' Jai said in a quiet voice, pointing to the sky

'Where is it darling? Where is Temper? I can't see ...'

'There it is Mummy! There it is Mummy!' Jai was so excited, he pointed his finger towards the light. 'Temper's right up to the sky ... look'.

Mummy looked up to where Jai's finger was pointing, 'Oh wow Jai!!! That's wonderful. How did Temper get up there?'

'I Threw Temper up to the sky' Jai demonstrated for his mum.

'Jai, you did so well, it is very high.' Mum sat down next to Jai, and Jai rested against her. They both were looking at Temper curiously.

'Hmmmm,' wondered Mummy, 'What colour is Temper?'

'It's blue,' Jai said immediately, 'It's a big blue.'

'Jai, that's so great! Do you feel better without Temper? or do you miss Temper?'

'Better Mummy.'

'Is that a good thing?' asked Mummy with a smile.

'Yes, it's a very good thing', Jai's smile glistened back to his mum.

'Would you like to tell Daddy how you got rid of Temper?' asked Mummy holding out her hand for Jai's

'Yes ...' and, as Jai was taking his Mummy's hand, he paused for a moment,

'And we have to tell Muffy too'.

About the story of temper
by Tracy Castelino

Jai and I wrote 'The story of Temper' together. I am Jai's mother. Jai is my child. He is nearly three years old. He has a passion for life, for enjoying every possible thing he does. His passion is sometimes snuck up on by this growling, grumpy, gripping temper. Temper hangs on Jai and talks him into all sorts of things - like hitting, kicking, yelling and grabbing. Temper causes problems for Jai and other people too.

I have been talking with Jai about temper since he was about eighteen months old. These conversations have not always been easy as Temper is sometimes very loud and rude. Jai and I have always managed to get rid of Temper though, even if sometimes it has only been for a little while.

We want to share our ideas with other Mums and Dads, other carers, but especially with other children who get caught by Temper as it can be tricky sometimes.

Temper found Jai as early as sixteen-eighteen months. I have been talking to him about feelings, and responses since I first held him, obviously more as he found words. When Temper gets a grip of Jai, it has been useful to talk with him about Temper's tricky ways:

- *What is Temper doing?*
- *How it is making you feel?*
- *How does Temper affect/hurt others?*
- *What could we do about Temper?*

Initially, I offered ideas to Jai like putting Temper in the rubbish bin or behind the couch, but before too long Jai's imagination opened many more ways of 'getting rid of Temper' such as catching temper and throwing it to the sky.

Jai and I also spoke about other people and their feelings and what we could do to help them feel better given that Temper was causing these problems. My adult mind, unknowingly locked into limited ways of recompense, only suggested saying sorry and maybe giving the other person a cuddle. Jai's creative mind has come up with many other helpful possibilities. After Temper has affected one of his friends, Jai has given flowers, made Wiggles pictures, helped others with the building blocks, and shared his special Winnie the Pooh toy so that Mitchell (his cousin) could have a cuddle 'that would make him feel better'.

Jai sometimes finds it difficult to throw Temper away especially when other children are playing with his blue guitar. He has been known, under the influence of Temper, to say, 'Mummy, I am very angry at Mitchell, I am going to kick him now ... and it will hurt'. After the initial social imperative of self-blame and awkwardness that clutch me as parent (due to the verbalisation of hurtful ideas by my child!!), I now find it possible to acknowledge in Jai's statement his connection to his feelings, his honesty, his competency in explaining his troubles, and the possibilities that are opened when he comes to me and talks *before* Temper has created trouble. Jai's security and honesty in speaking to me gives me the opportunity to share in his troubles and discuss alternative ways of managing Temper in the moment, as well as in the rest of his life.

At the moments when Temper is present, I have found holding Jai close, being at his eye level, and having a quiet, calm tone, can engage Jai in a conversation that strengthens him and challenges this culture's taken-for-granted power differential between adult and child. Asking questions and offering possible responses to Jai seems respectful of his sense of the situation. There are, however, continuing ethical dilemmas, especially where other children are involved. For instance, in discussing with Jai his choice whether or not to kick Mitchell for playing with his guitar, I might ask:

- *What would that be like for Jai?*
- *For Mitchell?*
- *For Temper?*
- *Who would be happy?*
- *Who would be sad?*
- *Would kicking make Temper the boss or Jai the boss?*
- *Does Temper being the boss cause more trouble for Jai?*

Of course, questions with Jai at this age often need to be qualified and not piled together. It is easy to continue to explain questions and ideas.

Sometimes the conversations themselves are not enough. For example, there have been times when Jai has said 'I don't want to throw Temper away!! I want to kick him and he will be hurt!!' In these situations Jai may not want to continue the conversation and the safety of another child could be at risk. At these moments I have held Jai, gone to another room and cuddled him, talking, waiting, holding him, till his passion and love quells Temper. Then we cuddle and talk about his skill and cleverness in getting rid of Temper, how he did it, what worked, and what we could do next time. Externalising the problem has allowed Jai to have a relationship with, and conversations about, this horrible Temper.

I have great hopes for collaborating with Jai about his life, his ideas and choices. Using 'I' does not acknowledge and honour the others who have built a community of care for, and because of, Jai including his father (David), his Nana and Poppy (Brenda and Walter), his Aunty Nessa and Uncle Martin, Michael (his very special grown-up friend), and quite a few others.

Just as we collaborate with Jai and with each other about opening up possibilities of being for him, Jai reciprocates daily, hourly, by the minute. Through his passion, his energy, his giggling smile, his amazing imagination, Jai has offered me new ways of being a mother, a friend, a playgroup Mum, and a social worker.

Together we strengthen each other. We can throw caution to Temper and its cohorts, and enjoy many Temper-free times.

Notes

1. First published in the 1999 Vol.1 *Gecko*. Republished here with permission.
2. Jai and Tracy can be contacted c/- 24 Spenseley St, Clifton Hill VIC 3068, Australia.

PART V

Sexual
Abuse

11

Taking a defiant stand against sexual abuse and the mother-blaming discourse[1]

by

Mary Freer[2]

This article is concerned with the experience of women when their children have been sexually abused. I am deeply interested in ways that social work practitioners and therapists such as myself, can respectfully create 'loud' spaces where women's voices can be heard. My hope is created by the belief that the space for new discourse exists in our thinking, our speech acts and in our practice.

In January 1995 I commenced a qualitative feminist research study to analyse the experiences of seven women following the sexual abuse of their child/ren by a male family member or close friend (Freer 1995). The focus of the study was consistent with research which reveals that 95% of the perpetrators of child sexual abuse are men (Finkelhor 1984). This article is based on a small part of that study. It is important to note that the words and experiences of the women that are reproduced in this article are not taken from the context of therapeutic conversations. It was not my intention to engage in any kind of therapy with any of these women. I set out to hear something of the experience of mothers following the sexual abuse of their children, and to discover if the dominant discourse of mother-blaming was reproduced in the experiences of these women.

Many negative and damaging long-held assumptions have been made about mothers of children who have been sexually abused. These beliefs and assumptions have been well documented and are in direct contradiction to the information gained during the interviews with this group of women. It was, however, clear from the interviews that the women were directly affected by these beliefs and assumptions. The interviews with these women and my current work with women following the sexual abuse of their children has led me to explore more carefully the myriad ways in which the discourse of mother-blaming is inscribed on women's lives and reproduced within our culture and, more particularly, within the culture of therapy.

It is my hope that this article goes some way to providing the seven women with the opportunity to articulate their experience of the sexual abuse of their children. It is only by gaining a more thorough understanding of the effects of sexual abuse on the non-offending parent (most often the mother) who assumes the responsibility for caring for the abused child, that therapists and social work practitioners will be in a position to develop a more sensitive practice framework. Therapeutic practitioners can take a defiant stand against mother-blaming practices. However, to do this we must attend to the ways that these dominant cultural ideas are reproduced in our work. When we note that a mother's response to her children is less than adequate, do we also note that our welfare system, our culture and our provisions for her are also less than adequate? This article is intended as an invitation to take a defiant stand against the mother-blaming discourse. It is my prediction that this stand will find us alongside our clients rather than in opposition to them.

It would be an understatement to say that professional literature has been unkind to mothers whose children have been sexually abused. Historically, the professional literature that describes child sexual abuse has been built on a foundation of misogyny, mother-blaming and excuse finding (McIntyre 1981). The most striking features of the literature are the invisibility of the perpetrator (Laing & Kamsler 1990) and the extremely narrow repertoire of roles assigned to the mother figure.

It would be comforting to rest in the knowledge that the most anachronistic and damaging ideas about women were abandoned in the 1950's along with the practice of describing women whose children were diagnosed as having schizophrenia as 'schizophregenic mothers'. Unfortunately family therapy in the 1980's was not immune to the discourse of patriarchal hegemony and continued to reproduce the idea of the 'dysfunctional family'. The view of families as dysfunctional is highly influential and informs our professional view of appropriate treatment programs for intervention where incest has occurred (Laing & Kamsler 1990). Giaretto (1982) describes the dysfunctional family as 'a family headed by two parents who are unable to develop a satisfying marital relationship and who cannot co-operate effectively as parents' (p.180). This discourse positions the occurrence of incest as being merely symptomatic of the 'dysfunctional family'.

The goal of family therapy according to Giaretto was to 'facilitate a harmonious familial system' (Giaretto 1982, p.190). In order for this to occur, both parents needed to admit their share in the responsibility for the incest occurring. Giaretto (1982) felt that incest was due 'in large part ... to a failing marriage for which both spouses are responsible' (p.195). Mothers needed to be educated and convinced that they shared in the responsibility for incest.

Kempe and Kempe (1978) supported the idea that women's withdrawal from their children and abandonment of their role as wife was the cause of incest. This abandonment theory positions women as the true perpetrators:

... most fathers who are incestuously involved with their daughters are introverted personalities who tend to be socially isolated and family oriented. Many, gradually sliding towards incestuous behaviour, are given the extra push by a wife who arranges situations that allow privacy between father and daughter. She may for example, arrange her work schedule so that it takes her away from home in the evenings, and tell her daughter to take care of Dad or to settle him down. It is not hard to see how a very loving and dependent relationship between father and

daughter may result first, in acceptable degrees of caressing and later in increasingly intimate forms of physical contact. (p.66)

Kempe and Kempe (1978) are dismissive of the idea that women are unaware of the abusive behaviour of their husbands/partners:

Stories from mothers that they 'could not be more surprised' can generally be discounted - we have simply not seen an innocent mother in long-standing incest, although the mother escapes the punishment that her husband is likely to suffer. (p.66)

Justice and Justice (cited in McIntyre 1981) arrived at six characteristics of non-participating' mothers:

1. they want to reverse roles with their daughters;
2. they are 'frigid' (sic);
3. they keep themselves tired or worn out;
4. they are weak and submissive;
5. they attempt to 'mother' their spouses; and
6. they are indifferent, absent or promiscuous.

These essentialist views of men and women, that have been popularised by professional writings over the last 30 years, are naive and one dimensional. Unfortunately they are also dominant and capturing. Breckenridge (1990, cited in Breckenridge & Bereen 1993) conducted research in New South Wales to determine the effect and prevalence of mother-blaming ideas on health and welfare workers. This research found that 10.3% of workers believed that a mother would know in most cases and 60.8% believed that a mother would know in some cases. Therefore, when dealing with mothers whose children have been sexually abused, (71.1% of workers believed), that these mothers (possibly) knew of the sexual abuse before the disclosure. Breckenridge and Bereen summarised this finding:

Whilst this knowledge does not in all cases equate with the mother's being held responsible for the abuse, it certainly indicates the view [held by workers] that mothers may have failed to act protectively towards their child. (1993, p.100)

Contextualising women's experience

The context for this article is a critical analysis of the practices and ideologies that have shaped our thinking and continue to maintain masculine hegemony throughout the professional literature and society. I believe that it is only from a standpoint that looks at the world through the eyes of those women who are subjugated by these assumptions and practices that we can observe and ask questions that cause us to re-examine perceived realities.

Harding (1991) has argued that all experiences and our interpretations of them are shaped by social relations. However, these social relations, as will be seen below, have primarily been from a dominant, patriarchal perspective. She illustrates this with the example of rape in marriage. Women did not always define those assaults that occurred in marriage as rape, rather they were seen as part of a range of heterosexual acts that wives should tolerate. The act of rape in marriage has not changed but women are now able to define this act as an assault. Harding put it this way:

> ... *it is not the experiences or the speech that provide grounds for feminist claims; it is rather the subsequently articulated observations of and theory about the rest of nature and social relations - observations and theory that start out from, that look at the world from the perspective of, women's lives.* (p.124)

In this same way, women's experiences of the sexual abuse of their children have been defined by social relations. The experiences that women spoke of in the course of the interviews must be seen for what they are; truly embedded in those same social relations and created by discourse (Featherstone & Fawcett 1994). Women's expressions of guilt and self-blame are examples of this influence. The continued focus on mothers by social welfare agencies, therapists and professional writers alike, has served to reinforce women's passivity (Mason 1989). In turn this focus deflects the attention away from the men who perpetrate sexual abuse on children and from '... the more intractable but central problem of masculinity' (Hooper 1992, p.11). Historically the attention given to these mothers has been damaging, and has generally not attempted to incorporate any analysis or empathic understanding of the women's subjective experience. A focus that validates women's experiences can act to empower all women.

Therefore, the context of this paper examines the experience of being a woman in a strongly patriarchal society where heterosexual masculine hegemony is pervasive in its subjugation of women. The concept of heterosexual masculine hegemony can be defined as those perceived practices of men and institutions that give them power, authority and privilege over others. These practices are multi-faceted and may include: the practice of heterosexuality; misogyny; homophobia; physical size; bodily strength and sexual violence (Blye 1995). It must always be remembered that hegemony is not a fixed notion and subscription to it is always optional.

Foucault (1979) has pointed out that every exercise of power, whether it is political or sexual will always generate some resistance or acquiescence on the part of those who are subjugated. The resistance and struggle of women to articulate their own subjective historical experience must be acknowledged within this context.

Social workers, in particular, play an important role in the delivery of services to these women. Social work is the profession that has been charged with the predominant responsibility for child protection. This responsibility carries with it the mandate to judge the safety of children and to assess the support that will be offered by the child's mother. In making these decisions it must be acknowledged that all professionals draw from a set of personal beliefs and values which are strongly influenced by prevailing 'mother-blaming attitudes'. One example of this is the scrutinisation of mothers by professionals when children's needs are not being met.

Deconstructing ideas about motherhood

There are a number of ideas relating to motherhood that operate through the socialisation process for women. They include mothering as a compulsory activity with the recruitment to this expectation beginning in infancy with the introduction of baby dolls. Mothering is seen as normative and the refusal or inability to bear children is considered deviant. Baber and Allen (1992) put it this way:

Messages about the importance and appropriateness of motherhood as a prerequisite for full womanhood are so clear and pervasive that they are almost impossible to escape, regardless of sexual orientation. (p.106)

However, the role of motherhood is shrouded in a mystique of dreamy, romantic language that acts to powerfully suppress the true patriarchal nature of mothering in our society. Women are defined by virtue of their willingness to bear and raise children. In addition, it is not sufficient for women just to desire to give birth and raise their children; these desires must be carried out within the confines of the heterosexual relationship. Women face rigid social sanctions if they seek to incorporate the role of mothering into a lesbian or single lifestyle.

Turner and Shapiro (1986) discuss the further influences of popular culture and peer pressure that coalesce to encourage women to remain in a relationship rather than face life as a sole parent or single woman.

... The emphasis on participating as a couple in social activities all combine to encourage women to feel more valued as partners than as individuals ... many women feel complete and fulfilled in a relationship but feel inadequate and lonely on their own. (Turner & Shapiro 1986, p.372)

Most women receive minimal training, support or payment to carry out the role of socialising the next generation. There is a certain expectation that women should not need to learn how to care for a newborn infant but rather that the arrival of lactation will herald the rush of maternal instinct. Despite this lack of support women are held almost entirely responsible for the behaviour and future successes or failures of their children and are expected to protect their offspring from harm or abuse. Failing this, they are required to engage their so called 'maternal instincts' in assisting them 'to know' if their children's safety is in jeopardy. A strongly pervasive attitude toward the sexual abuse of children, held by professionals and the public alike, can be summed up with the claim; 'a mother would know, **surely!**'

The women who share their experiences in this article took confusing and isolating journeys into health, welfare and legal services when they responded to their children's disclosure of sexual abuse. The hope of these women when they place their stories, their lives, in the public domain, is that they will make a difference to the dominant ideas that are at large about women just like them. Simone, one of the women interviewed put it this way:

> *You need Mums like myself to speak up, not just to our counsellors and our psychologists. But we need to be able to stand up in front of people who can do things and literally tell them 'This is what really happens, it doesn't just happen to someone else and you better damn well do something to help others!'*

The Disclosure

All the women[3] described feelings of shock and grief that accompanied the discovery that their child/ren had been sexually abused. Six of the women were able to recall the exact date and time that they were told about the abuse.[4]

Annette recalled the night that her four year old son Tom told her that he had been sexually abused by his grandfather:

> *I was driving along the road, my son was four then, he said 'I've seen Ken's penis' and I kind of went almost up a tree or something and we were almost at my sisters place at that stage, so I drove around the block a couple of times and just said 'how did that happen?' He just began to describe. I went to my sister's, more or less in a state of shock. I said 'You just won't believe what's just happened' and I burst out laughing. I thought 'My god, I'm hysterical, I'm going mad, I can't have heard that'.*

Following her son's later interview with a worker from a sexual abuse counselling service Annette came to hear the details of the abuse:

Kathleen's daughters are now in their early twenties. Both daughters revealed, while still in primary school, their experience of abuse by their grandfather.

Kathleen: *I didn't get the hint and I thought, it's alright you don't need to help me or do whatever, it's alright if you go* [with the grandfather]. *And my partner ended up approaching me and saying the reason they can't go is because this* [sexual abuse] *has happened in the past.*

Kathleen was faced with the memories of her own sexual abuse by her father and then the discovery that he had abused both her daughters.

Later, Kathleen's daughters disclosed to her that their step-father (Kathleen's partner) was also sexually abusing them. Kathleen described with continued pain and anguish the discovery that her partner had betrayed her.

Kathleen: *It's a bit like saying I've been to hell and back and you've decided you could still have power and effect in your life, in your space, so you go to do things differently and take control of your own life, so when something like this happens it almost negates everything. It feels like ... it's wiped out whatever control you thought you had. So I guess it can feel like the rat in the maze, every tunnel you try there's an electric shock at the end.*

Simone remembered clearly the exact details of how she found out her seventeen year old daughter had been sexually abused continually for the previous thirteen years:

Simone: *So I drove home and as I got out of the car a plain clothes policeman and two social workers, ladies, got out of another car a couple of cars down from where I pulled up and they stopped me on my front lawn before I went inside and they just said, 'There's no easy way to tell you this but there's police inside with your husband and they are about to arrest him and they are arresting him for sexual assault of your daughter'. So that was how I found out. It was really ... I guess I was just in shock because I didn't cry. I didn't do anything. I just wanted to get inside and see my daughter and then they told me that she wasn't there, she was somewhere else at the moment.*

Simone's husband was arrested moments later:

Simone: *... and my husband just looked up at me and said, 'I don't know what this is all about I haven't done anything. They want me to go to the police station.' And out they walked. I was left there with two counsellors and the police went with my husband. I can't really remember what we spoke about after they left, that's a bit of a blur. I just remember thinking I want my daughter to come home, I want her home, I want her home now.*

Briony's daughter was also seventeen when she disclosed her previous sexual abuse to her mother. Briony remembers the moment in this way:

Briony: *It came out of the blue, absolute bolt out of the blue ... I got home and my daughter was in tears, absolute floods of tears and I went to cuddle her and she said, 'No, don't. I just need to talk to you'. It's very unusual for her to be as emotional and then she led me through the house and said, 'Sit down outside', and said, 'I've got something awful to tell you'. I didn't know what it could be. She said she'd been abused by a partner that I had lived with for several years. We had separated about four years ago. I guess I was shocked but I also wasn't surprised it made sense to me.*

Briony's daughter went on to disclose that Briony's father had also sexually abused her:

Briony: *Then she said, 'but that's not all', and I thought 'what else!' Then she said that my father had abused her, that knocked me to the ground. I just could not believe that, I didn't disbelieve it but I just couldn't believe it. Three and a half years later I'm still working on that one. That was really what got me ... That really wiped me out. I didn't disbelieve her either.*

Mary: *Is it sort of being caught between not really being able to comprehend the truth of it but not doubting it either?*

Briony: *There's two levels, it's like how can this possibly be true but knowing deep down that it is. For the whole next week I was like a zombie. It was like the whole world was different. It was such a vivid experience. We talked for quite a while and she wouldn't tell me what happened and I still don't know the dates, well I have some idea. I spent 24 hours in tears, just in absolute shock. It was a hot day and I was shivering the whole time, that really cold feeling. I was trying to do things. I went to visit a friend and I'd see people and I felt totally unreal and I thought I can't go on like this.*

All seven women believed that their children were truthful in their disclosures. However, many of them were able to describe, as Briony did, that there are differing levels or phases of believing.

Suzi talked at some length about this aspect of disclosure:

It's like you can't imagine that she could say those things without it being true, she couldn't just make them up but he is so blankly denying that it possibly could have happened that it's like you've got two people telling you absolutely opposite stories about something really important. It's like who do I believe even though he'd proven that he was untrustworthy and she hadn't proven anything about her trust not being worthy of belief. I think there must be something in your brain that lets it slowly sink in ... that doesn't seem right though. That part is really difficult to describe because it took me quite a few weeks. I actually felt in the middle.

Six of the women interviewed used the term 'in shock' to describe their emotional state following the disclosure by their child/ren. The other woman used the term 'nightmarish'. Two of the women referred to the experience as similar to being in hell. The depth of painful feelings can be paralysing in their effects and result in serious emotional, mental and physical health risks to these women. It is clear, from these short excerpts alone, that women need empathic and supportive intervention following the disclosure of their child's sexual abuse.

Responding

You know that's one thing I feel really good about is that as soon as those words were out of Tom's mouth I went hysterical, I felt like a nutcase but I ACTED. I grabbed him and made him safe and get away from him you bastards, get out of here. And I was going to do whatever I had to do to keep him safe and to try to get him through it. So I feel really pleased about that. (Annette)

Following the shock of disclosure all seven women had to make some choices about how to respond. The contention of this article is that there is no one right way to respond. Some of the women who took part in the interviews were professionally trained workers in the welfare arena with expert knowledge about human services. Yet even these women discovered that their much valued skills were insufficient to prepare them for the confusing and distressing experience of disclosing their own child's sexual abuse to a maze of child protection agencies.

Decisions about who to tell and how to respond are best summed up by Clarissa:

I thought shit what do we do. I had no idea what to do. Do we let the police know? No, we don't want to waste their time. So we rang Crisis Care and they said we should ring the children's hospital. We rang the children's hospital and they said 'There's nothing we can do for you at this stage, ring at nine in the morning when the child protection unit is open'. They gave me a name.

Clarissa sat up all night and '... smoked about two packets of cigarettes and drank coffee ...' and waited until nine in the morning as instructed:

At five minutes to nine I got the phone out and thought what do I do, what do I do. So at nine on the dot I rang them and said 'My daughter's been abused, what do I do?'

The long wait through the night had devastating ramifications not only for Clarissa who had to endure a lonely night of anxious waiting but her child's swollen genitals were not photographed until much of the evidence was no longer visible.

Briony's seventeen-year-old daughter, Mandy, made it quite clear that she did not want police involvement, nor did she want other people to know what had happened to her. For Briony there were other issues to respond to :

... what I thought at the time was that Mandy needs to talk about this and I suggested that a few times but she said 'no, no, no'. About a week later I said 'Mandy I really think it would be useful to just give it a go' she said 'alright'. When I think about how difficult it was to find someone it makes me really angry. I really had so little knowledge about the whole area and so I just phoned up people left right and centre. [Every agency had a waiting list that Briony considered too long]. I couldn't find anyone. The whole process of trying to find someone took about a month.

Briony also wanted to see a counsellor to discuss what she described as a 'plan of action, a campaign' about how to cope with other family members:

I went to see the person who Mandy was seeing but I also knew this person in a professional sense, so we'd meet in other arenas and I realised that I felt uncomfortable with her. I picked up that she had been abused by her mother and that was sitting there between us ... I felt that blame somehow.

Kathleen chose to confront her partner following the discovery of her daughter's abuse:

Kathleen: [He] *denied it. I said 'don't give me that bullshit'. I was saying that but maybe not in those words. I was adamant, children don't make up these things. This is not made up... he then said it was true. What I ended up doing with him and with the girls actually was sitting with them and actually talking about what happened.*

Mary: *You sat with the girls and the person who had abused your daughters, the four of you talked about it?*

Kathleen: *Yeah. To clearly identify who was responsible and it was the perpetrator who was responsible. And have that person say 'it is my fault for what has happened'.*

Kathleen attempted to gain a commitment from her partner that the abuse would not occur again.

Mary: *How did you do that? How can you be sure of that?*

Kathleen: *... I took a risk ... I thought that because it's out in the open, because the person is accepting responsibility, because we're actually identifying a whole range of things, also what I did was I never went out at night again. I never left them. I figured that I could actually protect them. We did talk about prosecution, it wasn't an option that they wanted to proceed with.*

Tragically, Kathleen's partner did not honour his commitment and continued to sexually abuse Kathleen's daughters.

Annette responded by phoning the police and contacting welfare authorities. Annette's son Tom, who was then four years old was interviewed by police and gave a detailed and accurate statement which included the description of various guns that he had been threatened with. One of these guns Tom referred to as the 'elephant gun', this later turned out to be a rifle that Tom's grandfather had kept in his shed.

Annette: [The police] *couldn't find the [rifle], my mother had hid it. So they couldn't even charge him with weapons offences, because none of it was licensed. The pistols, my mother didn't even know that they existed, but there was a set of replica pistols which he [the grandfather] had been keeping for his son in the shed. So they found them and they were exactly as Tom described, but they were replicas, there was no offence. Tom didn't know they were replicas.*

Annette's son's case never went to court and his grandfather was never charged. However some time later Tom successfully applied for compensation and received $20,000 in accordance with the Criminal Injuries Compensation Act, 1978.

Simone put up surety for her husband's bail following his arrest. Simone continued to meet with her husband over the three weeks following the disclosure:

> *I'd meet somewhere and talk about it and try to question him, did he or didn't he? He kept talking about his innocence. But as I talked to both of them* [the husband and the daughter] *my head became quite clear. Later that year I actually confronted him and told him 'I believe* [our daughter] *and I told him that we wouldn't be getting back together ever'.*

Simone commenced seeing a psychologist and made arrangements for both her daughters [one of whom was not abused] to see separate psychologists. This placed an added financial strain on Simone's income.

In Simone's case her husband was arrested and charged for the sexual offences against his daughter. Sadly he was found not guilty and only served one night in custody. Simone remembers the court case with horror:

> *For me it was very, very difficult. I so desperately wanted to be in there with my daughter when she was giving her statement but I couldn't* [Simone was a witness in the case and therefore was not permitted in the courtroom while another witness, her daughter, was testifying]. *I found that very traumatic. I found it very traumatic that my husband* [the accused] *could walk in and sit in the same waiting room and stare at us, I would have thought it would have been kept separate ... I felt that the judge that we had quite blatantly is probably a child abuser himself and so obviously favoured my husband's defence to our prosecution. Even as far as when the questioning was going on he'd ask for clarification on minor matters ... the judge would actually speak up while the questioning was going on and re-question me personally. He'd question me in a way to make it sound as though it wasn't true. Yet when my husband was on the stand he'd question him as though he was a mate or something. I think that's so bad.*

Simone was not offered any professional support during the trial or afterwards, although she does recollect that on the night her husband was arrested two social workers gave her a copy of the book *Facing the Unthinkable* to read (Dympna House, 1990):

> *She* [one of the social workers] *gave me a book to read and her phone number. I did try and phone her once afterwards but she had moved on.*

Suzi remembers responding in this way:

> *I was in shock but I rang. I think Lucy's psychologist was away on holidays so I phoned the sexual assault services* [at a major hospital] *and they didn't treat children of Lucy's age so they referred me to the Child Protection Services and I said 'Should I be concerned about that?'* [meaning her daughter's disclosure]. *It seems silly to ask that now and they referred me to Family and Community Services. By this time it was five minutes to five and they said 'seeing as it's five minutes to five can you ring Crisis Care in five minutes'. So I waited and settled the children off to bed and phoned Crisis Care at nine that night.*

Suzi discovered that during the supervised access the children's father continued to deny to his daughter that he had abused her. On one occasion he told his daughter 'your mummy doesn't love you, she told me'.

> *I can't imagine what it must be like to have your father lie to you every time he sees you ... I can't imagine what it must be like to have to go and sit with a rapist for seven hours every fortnight.*

Suzi was advised by her solicitor not to speak with Lucy about the disclosure in case 'it contaminated the evidence'. Suzi did not speak about the abuse with her three year old daughter for ten weeks. At this stage Suzi decided along with Lucy's psychologist that it was not helpful to Lucy to be prevented from talking openly with her mother about her abusive experience. Suzi described her rationale for making the decision to go against her solicitor's original advice.

> *You can't have it all. You can't support your child in the short term because in the long term the court will just say you contaminated all the interviews. If you try to protect their long term interests, in the short term they have just told you this horrible secret and you can't be there to say 'isn't that awful'.*

Suzi chose a welfare agency and contacted them to arrange for ongoing therapy for her three year old daughter. Suzi felt that her daughter had been questioned and interviewed by various court and welfare professionals but had not received any counselling. After being told that the welfare agency she had chosen did not have a waiting list Suzi waited over six weeks for her telephone call to be returned and then decided to contact a psychologist in private practice. Suzi is paying, from her sole supporting parents benefit, for her daughter to consult with this psychologist on a regular basis.

Rose contacted a number of health and welfare agencies and finally located a social worker who was available to consult with her:

[The social worker] *did a lot of good and said things that made a lot of sense but she undermined it all by saying that my psyche had honed in on* [the abuser's] *psyche and brought him into our home and therefore it was my fault. I thought; you bitch. I am an adult survivor of sexual abuse and I had told her that and she said 'that's right you would have known he was a perpetrator of child sexual abuse and you have attracted him into your home'. When I got home after that I was just shot to pieces and I already blamed myself and I didn't need this woman who was in a paid professional position to be telling me it's my fault.*

The interviews with all seven women revealed that the issue of how to respond to the sexual abuse of your child is not a straightforward matter. Despite the array of professional services in place most women felt daunted in their task of locating the right service for their child.

Having found the 'right' service the women did not always find that their experience was treated respectfully.

Blaming

I soak it up, it's like something in the air that gets in the pores of your skin and you don't notice it until you start to feel sick. You soak it up ... all the attitudes towards women are just so real ... (Annette)

Six of the women interviewed experienced feelings of self-blame. Suzi was the only woman interviewed who had been able to resist critical self-blaming. Suzi believed that the absence of self-blame was unusual and put this down to her previous experience in a health and welfare agency, her feminist values and the strong support offered to her by friends. All seven women were subjected to blaming accusations by either friends, relatives and/or health and welfare workers. The women were all aware of dominant cultural stories that blame mothers for child sexual abuse. As Kathleen put it: 'There's a whole lot about mothers being totally responsible for most things in life so it totally fits'.

Clarissa had separated from her husband prior to her then two year old daughter, Louise's, disclosure of sexual abuse by a child care provider (Louise is now five years old). Clarissa felt that there is ongoing blame directed at her from a number of sources.

Clarissa: *I had my mother-in-law accuse me of it being all my fault because I chose the day care. My ex-husband accused me, it was my fault. He had a real hard time* [recently] *because I have started choosing schools for Louise and he said 'There's no way you're going to choose the school. Look at you, you're no judge of character. Last time you chose something look what happened!'*

Many of the women talked at some length about the value of hindsight.

Clarissa: *People said 'You should have known, why didn't you know?' A lot of symptoms that abused children display, especially when they are two, are normal behaviour problems for children anyway, so it's really hard to say 'Oh yes, my child's regressing with her toileting. She has to be abused!' Hindsight is always perfect. It was all there, it's a classic case with Louise, but you never think it's going to happen to you or your child. It's always going to happen to your next door neighbour. You never think it's going to be as bad as it is. It's like; that doesn't happen to two-year-old children.*

Simone had this to say about hindsight:

There are certain things I can think about now and I can say maybe something was happening ... in hindsight that's very easy to say. If you're not looking for it and you don't expect it, it's the last thing you think of. Do you know what I mean? So, yeah, there was probably evidence that it was going on but unless you were looking for it you wouldn't know, you wouldn't pick it up.

Kathleen has remained with her partner [one of the men who sexually abused her daughters]. Together, Kathleen and her partner have worked extremely diligently to address many of the issues that they believe are central to sexual abuse. Kathleen's commitment to her relationship with her partner is based on her partner taking total responsibility for the abuse. Kathleen talked about the decision not to live separately from her partner and became overwhelmed with sadness during the interview:

Mary: *Is it painful because when you revisit it you wish that the support had been there and other decisions could have been made?*

Kathleen: *Only partly that. It's a lot about because of what I know now. It's because of what I know in hindsight in terms of what is believed to be a good response.*

Mary: *And what's that? What is a 'good response'?*

Kathleen: *Mother gathering up her kids and running off into the sunset and getting the police to help. The sort of cavalier, well it is sort of a cavalier image of the right way to respond. I guess I feel a lot of shame and guilt. That's offset with the fact that I did the best I could then. It always remains a dilemma.*

Kathleen's daughters (who are now adults) are not accepting of their mother's decision to remain with her partner. One of Kathleen's daughters and the daughter's child have no contact with Kathleen and there remains ongoing anger and tension between them. Kathleen described the position of her daughters in this way:

I can't seem to, from whatever behaviour I take, I can't seem to undo what they perceive is my crime. Not behaving in the cavalier prescriptive way. I can list a myriad of ways in which I have acted appropriately to assist them, to defend them and to support them most fully ... in spite of that they still have decided that I have committed some terrible crime.

Annette had taken time off work because her son Tom was having behavioural problems. Annette's initial reaction to Tom's behaviour was to blame herself. It was some time before she discovered that ongoing sexual abuse was the cause of her son's anxiety:

He was in a child care centre and they were having problems with him and they had actually got him assessed by the psych and they said 'He's just a gifted child, he's very, very bright and he's not being challenged ...', kind of thing. They gave us some suggestions, the behaviour didn't improve. Being a single parent and all that stuff and I'd worked ever since he was really small therefore I'm a bad mother. My child is cracking up because I'm a bad mother and I don't spend enough time with him so therefore the career has to go on hold and I will spend twelve months at home with him. So that's what I did.

When Annette discovered that Tom was being sexually abused by his grandfather she blamed herself for allowing him to go to the grandfather's home:

I should have known this, I should have seen this coming. I should never have let him go.

Rose talked about the mother-blaming ideas that are held by professional workers and noted the invisibility of the role of the perpetrator:

People read things out of books and you believe what they say because these people are supposed to be learned people and all we are is mothers and housewives. They must know more than we do, therefore we're wrong. It really isn't like that. There is no blame on the perpetrator, which is where it should be. It shouldn't be the mother's fault. It shouldn't be 'you let him'. Like me, I used to let my son-in-law into my daughters' bedrooms. He said he was reading my youngest one a story and I believed him because I trusted him. I totally trusted him. I thought nothing more of it. When I found out what he had done I felt totally betrayed by someone who was my friend ... It really is bad, the parents feel so stupid. You feel so guilty. You feel like a 'dim wit' because you never twigged. I never thought; hey this man might be raping my daughter. I thought. 'Hey, he said he's going to read her a story so that's what he's doing'. It's disgusting they set up these webs. I always describe them as black widow spiders. They weave this magic web all over everybody and then they pounce.

Briony and Simone (both of whom had daughters who were seventeen at the time they disclosed their abuse) felt at times that their daughters blamed them for not knowing about the abuse prior to disclosure.

Briony: *After she told me there was a lot of animosity and hostility. She kept saying 'Look I'm not blaming you'. But I felt like they were just words really and underneath she did blame me for not being 'mum' and picking up about the abuse. It's kids' expectations that mum can protect.*

Simone described similar feelings:

Mary: *Do you think your daughter blames you?*

Simone: *One day I'll say she absolutely hates my guts and blames me for everything and another day I'll say she doesn't blame me at all. Then on another day I'll say she's trying to pay me back. So it's a hard question. It's emotional turmoil, backwards and forwards. Some days I feel that way and some I don't.*

The issue of blaming was raised many times throughout the interviews. It is all too easy for us to minimise the effect of blaming ideologies and accusations against women. These interviews reveal that women are subjected to blaming and are influenced by mother-blaming ideas. Given that the professional literature describing child sexual abuse has been built on a foundation of misogyny, mother-blaming and excuse-finding (McIntyre 1981), the experience of the women should come as no surprise. Indeed, many of the women spoke before the interview of their anxiety that I might choose to blame them also.

The Impact of the Abuse on Women's Lives

We are all too familiar with the effects of sexual abuse on the lives of the children who are abused, but what of the mothers who care for these children? Historically the literature has provided little insight in this area as it maintains the invisibility of the needs of these women. All the women interviewed felt that the abuse had a major impact on their lives. The women experienced a variety of negative effects of the abuse.

In Clarissa's case she was continually harassed by the abuser and was eventually forced to change her name and re-locate to a new address. Clarissa was able to describe the ways that her child's abuser had tried to terrorise her into silence:

> *I had cats go missing and come back with bits of fur shaved off. I had my pet rabbit baited. I had things stolen out of my backyard. I had my washing moved on my line. [The abuser] would sit at the end of my street. My car was broken into twice, never anything stolen just windows smashed and things messed around.*

Clarissa became understandably frightened to be alone and anxious in the company of others:

> *I lost 32 kilos in six months. I just didn't eat. I lived on coffee and cigarettes. I came very close to picking up the bottle. I slept maybe two hours a night. I just existed. You don't live. You don't have a life.*

Clarissa was also able to identify the socially isolating impact of spending her days moving from one appointment to the next, consulting with a myriad of professionally trained people. This continued focus on her daughter meant that Clarissa began to feel as though her entire purpose was to be the mother of her child:

> *I couldn't tell you what the weather was like or what I did. I can tell you exactly what Louise did. No idea what I did. I existed to care for her, to get her through it. I had a shower every day. I washed my hair every day and I brushed my teeth and that was life.*

Annette took twelve months leave from work without pay and subsequently was unable to cover her mortgage payments and was forced to sell her home. Three years after the sexual abuse Annette's son began to behave in a sexually inappropriate way at school. Annette felt shamed and humiliated by her son's behaviour and experienced a 'fear that he would grow up to be a child molester'. At around this time the strain of the preceding three years began to take its toll on Annette's health and she began to experience panic attacks and increasing feelings of despair. Annette felt that she could not care for her son and asked her mother to take him - he remained in his grandmother's care for five months:

> *I just thought I can't go on. I couldn't stand another minute I was so sad it*

was just awful. At that point I was firmly convinced that although we might have got through the initial crisis I was still a dreadful mother and shouldn't have this child and I should give him away. I should have him adopted, he should go away. So I actually rang the adoption services to find out how to do this.

Annette described the impact of those five months as 'socially isolating' and believes that the effects of that isolation continue four years later. Annette did not give her son up for adoption and now believes that they have forged a far stronger relationship because of the abuse. This is in direct contrast with much of the literature which suggests mother-child relationships are irreparably damaged following child sexual abuse.

Simone took five weeks off work at around the time of her daughter's court case. When she returned to work she was informed that the company was being restructured and her position as General Manager was no longer required. After initially trying to persuade Simone to take a short contract position overseas the company tried much tougher tactics to get rid of her:

One of the Directors approached me and said that the company had lost total confidence in me and I didn't have a job any more. I felt it was totally uncalled for. I'd had quite a bit off time off work, naturally, but I hadn't done anything at work to cause them to dismiss me. That was the second most traumatic thing that's ever happened to me.

Briony's comments reflect most closely the ongoing experience of all the women interviewed:

I don't get upset about it now like I used to. The periods between being angry and frustrated have lessened or they are not as intense ... I think it is something that will live with us forever. What I hope is that we will recognise what we have learnt from it too. We are much stronger people I'm sure.

Some conclusions

The stories of these women are in stark contrast to much of the previously published ideas about women whose children are sexually abused.

These women are not the jealous, manipulative and ineffectual women as the literature would have us believe. Far from being 'dysfunctional', these women were striking in their courage and honesty.

It is my hope that this article goes some way to providing these women with a platform to articulate their experience and perceived needs. It is only by gaining a more thorough understanding of the effects of sexual abuse on the non-offending parent (most often the mother) who assumes the responsibility for caring for the abused child, that therapists and social work practitioners will be in a position to develop a more sensitive practice framework.

Therapeutic work and social work intervention must reflect far more sensitive practice which is based on our understanding of the experience of these women and not on the masculine hegemonic ideology of our culture. If it is the case that we want to make a defiant stand against the seductive power of mother-blaming practices, then we must begin to attend to the ways that these dominant cultural ideas are reproduced in our work. If we were to externalise mother-blaming as a powerful and alluring force that sought to capture our attention then we might be more equipped to take a personal and political stand against this discourse.

If we were to take this stand then we might find ourselves in closer proximity to the struggle of our clients, who are often labouring under the weight of self-blame and guilt. To refuse to blame women for the sexual abuse that is perpetrated by men against children is not to ignore the experience of children when their mothers are unable to support them. The experience of sexual abuse as a child is so painfully devastating that I would not be able to find sufficiently sensitive words to describe it. To endure this experience in isolation, without the support of your non-offending parent could be experienced as annihilation. To **refuse** to entertain the discourse that invites us to disperse the responsibility for the immensity of this experience on the mother, is to create new ways of working with women and their children.

In conclusion, it is important that we remember that women's lives are full of events that come together to give meaning and sense to the experience of being a woman in our culture. The women who participated in these interviews were striking in their courage, honesty and ability to create respectful relationships with their children despite the abuse. In their act of bravery these women have stood up to '... the truth making power of patriarchy' (Laird 1994).

Acknowledgements

I would like to thank the seven women with huge reservoirs of courage and insight, who took part in this research project and collaborated in the writing of this article. Over the years since the initial publication of this paper many people have offered their comments to me. It is because of the continuing dialogue that this paper seems to encourage that I offer it again for publication.

Notes

1. First published in the 1997 Vol.1 *Gecko*. Republished here with permission.
2. Mary Freer currently works as the Director of a Women's Health Centre in Adelaide. Prior to Mary's involvement in management she worked as a Community Health Worker and was mainly involved in providing counselling to women who had experienced the effects of men's violence and abuse on their lives. Mary can be contacted c/- Women's Health Statewide, 64 Pennington Tce, North Adelaide 5062, South Australia.
3. The women were given an opportunity to re-read their own words and decide if they wanted to be involved in this project. Some of the women elected to express themselves slightly differently for this public context. These new expressions will differ in places from the original transcripts (reproduced in Freer 1995).
4. All names and identifying information has been changed to protect the identity and safety of these women and their children.

References

Baber, K.M. & Allen, K.R. 1992: *Women and Families: Feminist reconstructions.* New York: Guildford.

Blye, F. 1995: 'Masculinity and schooling: Educating for 'real' men.' *South Australian Educational Leader*, 6(2).

Breckenridge, J. & Bereen, R. 1993: 'Dealing with mother-blame: Workers' responses to incest and child sexual abuse.' In J. Breckenridge & M. Carmody, (eds), *Crimes of Violence: Australian responses to rape and child sexual assault.* NSW: Allen & Unwin.

Dympna House Editorial Writers Collective 1990: *Facing the Unthinkable: A guide for mothers whose children have been sexually abused.* NSW: Dympna House.

Featherstone, B. & Fawcett, B. 1994/95: 'Feminism and child abuse: Opening up some possibilities?' *Critical Social Policy*, 14(3).

Finkelhor, D. & Russell, D. 1984: 'Women as perpetrators.' In D. Finkelhor (ed), *Child Sexual Abuse: New Theory and Research.* New York: The Free Press.

Foucault, M. 1979: *The History of Sexuality.* London: Allen Lane.

Freer, M. 1995: *Unspeakable Realities: The experience of women whose children have been sexually abused.* University of South Australia: Unpublished Honours Thesis.

Giaretto, H. 1982: *Integrated Treatment of Child Sexual Abuse.* Palo Alto, CA: Science and Behaviour Books Inc.

Harding, S. 1991: *Whose Science? Whose Knowledge? Thinking from women's lives.* New York: Cornell University Press.

Kempe, R.S. & Kempe, C.H. 1978: *Child Abuse.* London: Fontana.

Laing, L. & Kamsler, A. 1990. 'Putting an End to Secrecy: Therapy with mothers and children following disclosure of child sexual assault.' In M. Durrant & C. White (eds), *Ideas for Working with Sexual Abuse.* Adelaide: Dulwich Centre Publications.

Laird, J. 1994: 'Changing Women's Narratives: Taking back the discourse.' In L. Davis (ed), *Building on Women's Strengths: A social work agenda for the twenty first century.* New York: Haworth Press.

Mason, J. 1989: 'In whose 'best interests'? Some mothers' experiences of child welfare interventions.' *Australian Child and Family Welfare*, 14(4).

McIntyre, K. 1981: 'Role of mothers in father-daughter incest: A feminist analysis.' *Social Work*, November.

Turner, S.F. & Shapiro, C.H. 1986. Battered women: Mourning the death of a relationship.' *Social Work*, Sept-Oct.

12

Liberation from self-blame:

Working with men who have experienced childhood sexual abuse[1]

by

Patrick O'Leary[2]

Introduction

This paper explores ways of working with men who have experienced child sexual abuse. It explores some of the difficulties that these men may face in our current social, political and cultural context. The paper explores the practical implications of the fact that male sexual abuse occurs within a male-dominated culture and that the large majority of perpetrators are other men. It describes how, for men who have been subject to sexual abuse, dominant constructions of masculinity can contribute to the silencing of their experience and to stories of self-blame. It explores the complex task that males who have experienced abuse from older men face in creating their own preferred masculine identity, and describes a number of therapeutic themes that I have found helpful in working with men on these issues.

At the outset I wish to acknowledge that within this paper I write from the position of a professional therapist working with men who have experienced childhood sexual abuse with all of the responsibilities that this brings. I want to be clear that there are some invitations of professionalism that I wish to decline. I have tried not to place survivor's speech at the mercy of detached theory and observation. I have tried not to imply at any point that helping professionals know something about survivors' experience that survivors themselves do not know. Like many people who have taken the position of a professional role in speaking up for those who have experienced sexual abuse, I have my own personal reasons for doing so. I -feel strongly that no one can represent the experience of all those who have been affected by child sexual abuse. The work described in this paper has primarily been informed by conversations I have shared with men about their experiences of childhood sexual abuse. I have a commitment to honouring their expertise. As Alcoff & Gray (1993, p.282) describe: *We need to transform arrangements of speaking to create spaces where survivors are authorised to be both witnesses and experts, both reporters of experience and theorists of experience.* I hope that this paper contributes to such a proposal. I invite critique of the ideas within this paper and look forward to hearing people's feedback.

Background

Inquiries carried out by women involved in the most recent wave of the women's movement into the prevalence of childhood sexual abuse in western countries have resulted in indications of the extent of abuse experienced by both female and male children. Although definite figures are impossible to ascertain, it is now clear that sexual abuse occurs to both female and male children in substantial numbers.[3] With the extent of the problem becoming more acknowledged, women workers, writers and researchers over the last twenty years have developed a substantial body of literature on childhood sexual abuse. Primarily this work has focused on female victims. We as men seem to have been much slower to respond to the knowledge of the sexual abuse of male children.

Recently this has begun to change. Men's experience of childhood sexual abuse has begun to gain prominence, and a body of knowledge concerning the issue is now being developed.[4] Certain male writers have recently claimed that the reason the issue of male childhood sexual abuse has been silent for so long is due to, of all things, feminism and that it has been the 'Men's Movement' which has brought the issue to light.[5] This does not ring true to me. In my experience, the primary initiative to respond to male victims of sexual abuse has come from women researchers, such as Nasjleti (1980) who, in advocating for greater attention to the sexual abuse of female children, noted that the occurrence of male victims had been severely underestimated.[6] What's more, it has been the work of women that has enabled abuse to be able to be talked about, and it is generally the women in men's lives who have supported them to address their experiences of abuse.

It is my experience from working with men who have experienced childhood sexual abuse, that 'the speaking out and naming of sexual abuse' by the women's movement has made it far more possible for these men to come forward. Feminist writers and therapists in their liberation work with women who have been subjected to abuse, are probably having the greatest direct and vicarious impact on the uncloaking of the occurrence of sexual abuse against males. From my practice experience the effect of this liberation appears to be particularly resonating with young men. It appears that the social change in the 1970s and 1980s has created the possibility for men who grew up in these eras to disclose experiences of abuse.

Still it is hard for many men to find a safe context to speak of their own experience of sexual abuse. The majority of men who are demonstrating a willingness to disclose abuse, as in many areas of men's health, are often seeking counselling at a point when the issues they are facing have become intensely serious and they feel they are out of control. It is often the partners or mothers of these young men who are making the initial request for counselling on the man's behalf. Often these men have had contact with other human service agencies in relation to various issues or occurrences, for example, a suicide attempt, the use of alcohol and drugs, a relationship break-up, issues of anger and violence, experiences in the juvenile justice or prison system, the birth of their first child, or struggles they are having with mental health issues. By the time these men are referred to our service they have generally already disclosed experiences of sexual abuse. How we as professionals respond depends upon our theoretical understandings.

Theoretical understandings

In order to respond to men who have experienced child sexual abuse it seems important to understand the effects of childhood sexual abuse on their lives. The effects of childhood sexual abuse seem to depend upon two separate factors. Firstly, the trauma associated with the actual event or events and the manipulation experienced from the perpetrator. Secondly, and perhaps more importantly in relation to the ongoing effects of abuse, are the meanings that are made of the abuse by those who have been subject to it. These meanings are greatly influenced by the broader cultural understandings of gender and power, and beliefs associated with the attribution of responsibility.

People who are subjected to childhood sexual abuse make meaning out of these events. These understandings that they generate and/or are recruited into in relation to the abuse often impose negative implications for how they define and express themselves in life. Often these understandings involve a belief that something about themselves or their actions was central to the abuse occurring, as White (1994, p.83) describes:

> *These understandings invariably feature themes of culpability and unworthiness; that somehow the person deserved the abuse or had it coming to them, or could have stopped it if they really wanted to.*

People who experience abuse and are recruited into negative stories about themselves may often be involved in self-destructive and self-abusive behaviours that more or less confirm their negative understanding and definition of themselves. These ways of being can then become central to how they construct reality and their identity.

This process of recruitment into negative understandings of their lives and actions can occur for both females and males who have experienced childhood sexual abuse. There are however, I believe, significant differences in the experience of females and males due to the dominant construction of gender relations in this culture. Many writers have documented how the experience of sexual abuse for women occurs within the context of patriarchy and the effect that this can have on making meaning out of the abuse.[7] Here I wish to focus on how gender relations and dominant constructions of masculinity can affect the ways in which men respond to the experience of sexual abuse. More particularly, I wish to focus on the ways in which dominant constructions of masculinity can contribute to the silencing of experience and to stories of self-blame.

Locating the sexual abuse of males within the broader context of patriarchy

Despite the achievements of the women's movement, men's violence and control in the private sphere still threatens so many homes, and men's ways of being in the public sphere continue to shape our culture in ways that deny alternative experiences, voices and ways of being. I believe that it is important to acknowledge that the sexual abuse of male children and adolescents occurs within a male-dominated culture. This seems important not only for ethical reasons but because the ways in which masculinity is understood has a profound effect on therapeutic practice with males who have been subject to sexual abuse. An understanding of men's power and privilege can lead to explorations of the dominant constructions of masculinity. In turn this can provide important avenues to explore with male survivors of sexual abuse.

I also believe that it is important to acknowledge that the sexual abuse of males (as with females) is predominantly perpetrated by older men. This is not to deny the existence of abuse of young males by women - especially as the reporting of such occurrences seems to be increasing.

It is, however, an important acknowledgement because it makes the link between childhood sexual abuse and dominant constructions of masculinity. It also creates space to begin to explore the complex task that faces males who have experienced abuse from older men in creating their own preferred masculine identity.

Elsewhere writers have described the ways in which the maintenance of inequitable gender relations depends upon the maintenance of dominant constructions of masculinity.[8] Dominant constructions of masculinity privilege a particular blueprint of manhood, and set certain criteria for male experience and behaviour. These criteria, which vary across history and culture, refer to personal characteristics and ways of being. In present day Australia, despite recent challenges, dominant constructions of masculinity still dictate to a large degree that men should be unemotional but logical; independent; hard but fair; benevolent but not vulnerable; physically strong; attractive to women; sexually dominant, and so on.

Dominant constructions of masculinity influence personal characteristics and ways of being as well as significantly influencing ways of relating with women, children and other men. Notions of male superiority to women, of adults' power over children, and of heterosexual dominance and homophobia, conspire within the dominant constructions of masculinity to influence relationships between men, women and children.

These dominant notions of manhood go a considerable way in explaining the extent of sexual abuse in our culture. They also shed light on the difficulties that male survivors of childhood sexual abuse may experience. The dominant constructions of masculinity have many ramifications for males who have been subject to childhood sexual abuse. Here I will discuss just three.

1. Males are not supposed to be 'victims'

Male victims of childhood sexual abuse are caught in a paradox of sorts. By the fact of their gender they are a member of a dominant group. Yet experiencing violation in the form of abuse goes against the membership of this privileged group and contradicts dominant men's ways of being. The result can often be a resounding silence and a recruitment into feeling 'less than a man'. Dominant constructions of male identity often serve to further recruit males who have been subject to abuse into understanding the abuse as a problem within themselves.

Within dominant constructions of masculinity, certain ideas prevail that victimisation is the outcome of deficiency. These ideas can reverberate intensely in relation to sexual abuse, beyond deficiency to inferiority and compulsion. Complex notions of masculine identity - which are themselves bound up in the construction of inequitable gender relations - can result in males who have been subject to abuse experiencing profound self-blame, as Mendel (1993, p.25) describes:

... the failure to protect seems entirely internalised: the men in this study experience themselves as deficient, unmanly, and incompetent because they could not provide themselves with adequate protection against abuse. The sense of self-blame is exacerbated by the 'myth of complicity', as Gerber

(1990) terms it, in which the male victim assumes he must have been an active, willing participant in his childhood sexual activity. The message to the male victim is not simply that if he was abused he must not be a man, but also that if he is a man he must not have been abused.

2. Homophobia & heterosexual dominance

Homophobia and heterosexual dominance can be further agents for secrecy and confusion. Confusion about sexuality is often a common effect for males who have been subject to child sexual abuse. Young men are particularly vulnerable to being recruited into a questioning of their sexuality based on another person's abusive acts. A story is often created by those perpetrating the abuse in which a disclosure will result in a questioning of the young man's manhood, and assumptions about his identity. This can greatly contribute to the silencing of their experience.

For young men in the process of constructing their own sexual identity, to experience men's sexuality as an oppressive force can have long-term consequences. Where the perpetrator of abuse has been a man, finding a way through the complexities of separating abuse from same-sex contact, and standing up to reactions of homophobia at the time of disclosures can be profoundly confusing.

Young men who have been subject to sexual abuse and are trying to establish or re-establish their sexual identity, can also be influenced by heterosexual dominance in ways that impact upon others. Dominant constructions of masculinity invite young men to obtain membership of their male peer group through demonstrating homophobic actions and actions that are based on ideas of male sexual entitlement to women.[9] For male survivors of sexual abuse, finding a way through these issues can be enormously complex.

3. From victim to perpetrator

A further complication for males in their attempts to address the effects of childhood sexual abuse is the link often made between being a victim of sexual abuse and being a perpetrator of abuse. Various research studies have shown that many sex offenders have experienced childhood sexual abuse. However, this evidence in no way proves causality; nor does it prove that it is in any way more likely for males who have experienced abuse to become perpetrators of abuse; nor does it in any way indicate that perpetrating childhood sexual abuse is dependant on prior victimisation. Furthermore, the data indicates that most males who experience childhood sexual abuse do not go on to sexually offend.[10]

The ways in which the connection between sexual victimisation and later sexual offending are comprehended by the community as exemplified by how the issue is publicised, with the media citing simple explanations for complex problems. Many elements of the mainstream media have given the impression that a male who is sexually abused is likely to become a sex offender. And yet the vast majority of males who suffer childhood sexual abuse do not go on to become sex offenders. Promoting the construction of 'Victim to Perpetrator' is not strictly valid. What's worse is that it is restrictive and potentially self-fulfilling.

Exploring the effects of sexual abuse and the association between victimisation and offending seems important. However, how can we ensure that we remain aware of the effects of the questions we ask, the research we promote? How can we keep in touch with how our explorations impact on the people affected by sexual abuse?

To pathologise sexual abuse as a 'cycle of violence' is to run the risk of obscuring personal agency. It is to run the risk of becoming complicit with ideas of biological determinism. Furthermore, it can unwittingly support the dominant constructions of male sexuality that imply that men are not in control, nor responsible for, their sexual impulses.

For males who have been subject to childhood sexual abuse, the need to deconstruct ideas about becoming a perpetrator can be important. This can be made more difficult by therapeutic approaches that contribute to metaphors of 'being wounded', or being 'damaged goods'. These metaphors can unwittingly contribute to pathologising practices, to self-blame, and to feelings of powerlessness in relation to moving from 'victim to perpetrator'.

Thinking about ways to have conversations with men who have experienced child sexual abuse

By the time people disclose an experience of abuse they have often been silenced for a significant time. When they do speak out they are then vulnerable to many types of scrutiny. This scrutiny may have the purpose of disproving and disbelieving the story, it may simply be testing the credibility of the story, or it may be a scrutiny constructed in a way that changes the meaning of the story. Some forms of scrutiny construct the act of speaking out as a 'confession'. In subtle ways, people who have experienced abuse may be seen as having to 'own up', 'face up' or 'show themselves for real' - in other words, confess.

There are a number of dangers in situating survivor speech in a confessional discourse structure (see Alcoff & Gray 1993). For one thing, to confess by its literal meaning is to admit to some level of culpability. But there are also some more complex repercussions. Just as the act of confession is linked to absolution, so too can the act of disclosure become seen as essential to achieve resolution or recovery. What is missed in this assertion is that the choices people make whether to disclose or not, who to tell, and more importantly who not to tell, are in themselves choices and acts of survival and resilience. Emotional, financial and physical difficulties can result from disclosures, and these problems in some circumstances can be seen to critically outweigh the support a person may receive should they disclose (Alcoff & Gray 1993, p.281). In my own experience, men have chosen only to disclose to a select person or persons and myself. This is because of the perceived risks, the jeopardy of their personal, social and professional lives, and the fear of the likely attribution made by others that the disclosure somehow 'explains everything'. How can we ensure that we respect people's decisions and resist the temptation to suggest that they will need to 'come clean' one day? How can we ensure that as therapists we are never in the position of 'absolver'? After all, what do survivors of sexual abuse or other abuses of trust have to confess to?

The following therapeutic themes are based on an acknowledgement that sexual abuse is an attack. In my experience, understanding sexual abuse as an attack which people resist, can allow for people's stories to be deconstructed and reconstructed in the process of therapeutic conversations. It can allow men who have experienced childhood sexual abuse to take a position of standing against the effects of the abuse as well as against dominant ideas about men's ways of being. I believe that situating sexual abuse as an attack places men's experience in a different context, one which limits the possibility for survivor's stories to be located within a confessional discourse, and one which creates the possibility to unfold what strength and courage can accomplish - namely liberation from self-blame.

These themes or principles are not listed in any particular order. They are ideas that have been helpful in my joining with men to name abuse and liberate from self-blame. They operate simultaneously with the men I consult with and, as such, they can often be used interchangeably from the early consultations to the latter. Where I have used examples of people's stories these have not been developed from specific individuals. They are stories which encapsulate many stories I have been witness to. The approach is not prescriptive. Particular themes are introduced according to the needs of the individual therapeutic journey. Some principles may not be helpful to individuals, and ways of questioning may often need to be modified to suit an individual's needs.

Naming the strategies of 'silencing', honouring what it takes to survive when silenced, and acknowledging the courage it takes to speak.

I believe that it is important to acknowledge that, when men attend counselling to address experiences of childhood sexual abuse, they are making a stand *against* the prevailing ideas of manhood and *for* alternative ways of being. These alternative ways of being are often informed by notions of caring, compassion and justice for themselves and for others. In my experience, it can be helpful in the initial counselling session to acknowledge the restraints that men and young men face in attending counselling. Men might be grappling with their own surprise that they have spoken out about the abuse. They may also have a number of internalised stories informed by self-blame as to why the abuse occurred. In the initial meeting with a man who has been subject to sexual abuse, I put significant energy into talking about the restraints of men's dominant ways of being and how these restraints can make attending counselling more difficult.

One small but significant step involves taking part of the responsibility for naming abuse by initially acknowledging the reason for the man's attendance. Naming childhood sexual abuse early in the conversation is an important step in taking a stand against the silencing of male disclosure of sexual victimisation. It helps to guard against men being in a position in which they feel they have been hiding something, and interrupts any chance of the conversation entering a confessional discourse (see Alcoff & Gray 1993). By naming the abuse myself this can often lead to conversations about the silencing of abuse and the man's experiences of this. I have found the following questions open space for helpful conversations on this topic:

- *What is it about the sorts of conclusions other people make about abuse that has made it hard for you to speak of your experiences?*
- *What is it about the ways in which men are 'supposed to be' that has made it hard for you to speak of your experiences?*
- *When you knew it wasn't safe to name your experiences of abuse and you had to remain silent, what was it that enabled you to get through?*
- *What does this say about your own internal strength?*
- *Would this fit with a story of weakness or a story of courage?*
- *What messages do you think it might give people if they knew we were talking about this issue?*
- *In choosing to talk about the abuse, could this mean that you are beginning a process of standing against the abuse?*

Conversations can develop from these sorts of questions that allow the man to position himself in overt ways against the effects of abuse. These conversations promote an acknowledgement of stories of strength and self-protection in the man's response to the experience of abuse.

Unmasking the politics of power[11]

Recruitment into self-blame often relies upon a denial of the power imbalances inherent in situations of abuse. Many men who have been subject to abuse have been recruited into a story that states that they should have been able to stop the abuse through physical or other means. It is not uncommon for men to be looking back at themselves as a ten-year-old thinking that they should have stopped a thirty-year-old man from abusing them. It is also common for men to have internalised a story of weakness in relation to the way they responded as a child to the abuse. Additionally, some men have been recruited into attributing the occurrence of the abuse to some behaviour or characteristic that they displayed as a child.

All of these stories of self-blame rely in some way on a denial of the abuse of power to which the child was subjected. Conversations that expose relations of power - both generally in relation to adults' authority over children, and specifically in relation to the acts of the perpetrator of abuse - can be freeing of self-blame. We explore the ways in which abuse becomes possible due to relations of power, through the use of manipulation, 'trickery' and privilege that works to cloud children's experience. Through exposing aspects of abusive thinking a number of therapeutic conversations can evolve.

We expose the manipulations of those who abuse. For example, one young man I was consulting with spoke about how the man responsible for the abuse would say to his mother, 'Isn't he a lovely kid? He is so affectionate, he's always wanting to sit on my lap.' Another young man described how his uncle suggested his sexually abusive behaviour was connected to the fact that the young man would walk through the house with only a towel around him.

A further tactic of power that is often articulated involves the ways in which the abuse has been named. Often the ways in which males have come to understand experiences of childhood sexual abuse have been influenced by the perpetrator's description of meaning which has mystified the tactics of abuse. One common term used for this mystification is 'mucking about'. In some situations this understanding can become aligned to self-blame, as it positions the abuse as interactional and fails to acknowledge the power imbalance.

Creating a context in which men can separate themselves from interactional understandings of the abuse and in which they can name their experience is an important part of the process. It involves great care, however, in order to ensure that as a counsellor I am not simply imposing yet another meaning upon their experience. The following sorts of questions can facilitate these conversations:

- *I know that the man who abused you told you that the sexual abuse was 'a bit of mucking around', but I also remember in our conversations you speaking about your experience of fear and shock at his actions towards you. Does fear and shock fit with 'mucking about' or would there be a more fitting description?*

- *What would this description be?*

- *Would this description make it more or less possible for you to move away from self-blame?*

Exposing the strategies of power and creating a context so that the abuse can be named enables a greater understanding about abuse and those who abuse. In these conversations it is often articulated how those who abuse look for opportunities to abuse; construct meanings that justify their own desires and actions; mystify their actions; and place responsibility for their actions on the young person. This process makes more visible the responsibility that adults have to children and adolescents. It allows for an understanding that the sexual abuse occurred due to the actions of the adult and how these actions occurred within a broader context of children's powerlessness. This sets the scene for standing against self-blame and valuing child, adolescent and adult ways of coping.

Disempowering 'self-blame' and honouring alternative stories

When people present to counsellors about their experiences of abuse they more often than not bring with them a story of culpability - a belief that they in some way were responsible for the actions of the perpetrator of the abuse. They have often been recruited into believing that their own ways of being were central to being abused or to the abuse continuing. This ought not to be too surprising. Recruiting the victim into a sense of responsibility for the abuse is often an important strategy that enables abuse to continue. In response to this situation, a central part of the therapeutic response is to externalise 'self-blame', to explore its effects and tactics, and to create opportunities for honouring hidden or devalued stories about the individual's response to the abuse. These stories have often been overtly or covertly interpreted by others as maladaptive or deficient. Reclaiming these stories and the preferred interpretations of them is an important aspect of this work. Four types of alternative stories have come to light in my consultations with men who have experienced sexual abuse as children: stories of protest, resistance, resilience, and connection.

1. Stories of protest

Stories of protest can often be found amongst stories of self-blame. Ben, in speaking of his experience of the abuse, shamefully acknowledged how he cried during the abuse and how he saw this as pathetic. He spoke of how he had questioned why he didn't as an eleven-year-old fight off a thirty nine-year-old man. These statements of self-blame could perhaps also be seen as an invitation to honour tears as protest. The following questions served to open this possibility:

- *What do you think an adult might make of an eleven-year-old crying?*
- *Would crying be an approval of what is happening to the child?*
- *What would it take for a thirty-nine-year-old man to ignore a child's distress and continue his actions?*
- *If crying was not an approval does that have it fit better with a protest?*

From questions like these a conversation can begin to construct a story of protest.

2. Stories of resistance

Men who have experienced sexual abuse often relate stories of how their identities have been constructed by others as 'juvenile delinquent' or 'anti-social teenager'. An example of this is where an adolescent might fail to attend family functions or truant from school because this might be the location where the abuse occurred or where the perpetrator may be present. Whereas these actions have in the past been construed as pathology or weakness, they can alternatively be understood as acts of resistance.

George, for example, spoke of how as a teenager he had been sexually abused by a teacher. He spoke of how he refused to go to school, and of how when at school he would smoke and not be complicit with school rules. He spoke of how this resulted in him being suspended and eventually expelled. He had never spoken about the abuse at the time. Due to his behaviour he was described in terms such as unco-operative, delinquent, lazy, and having no future. He internalised these descriptions.

Hidden stories of courage and resistance quickly surfaced in response to the following questions:

- *When you spoke of your experience of being silenced, do you think that this influenced you to make some other sort of statement like challenging rules?*

- *Would your actions of 'rebellion' at school have been more or less likely if the abuse had not of occurred?*

- *Did these actions of rebellion have you thinking it was more or less likely the abuse would continue?*

- *If this is so, would your actions be more fitting with laziness or more fitting with resistance?*

Stories of resistance became increasingly open to George as conversations informed by these sorts of questions continued.

3. Stories of resilience

Further avenues for the exploration of stories of survival are often found in men's solitary pursuits. In my experience men often speak about the games they played alone, or their imaginary friends who allowed them to escape into a world of their own. Over the years these experiences may have been interpreted by others to construct a negative story about themselves of being a 'loner' or a 'dreamer'. Once explored more fully, however, these experiences of solitary pursuits often become more available to support stories of resilience - stories of how they kept themselves sane and safe.

Philip, for example, who was abused by his older brother, described how as a child he would often play on his own for hours in an old car-wreck. He would spend hours imagining that he was a racing car driver who was having to make up lost ground. On each occasion he would eventually come from behind and win the race on the last lap. Philip spoke of how he had internalised other family members' views of his intelligence. He retold accounts of his brother taunting his ways of surviving with phrases such as 'small things amuse small minds'. In my conversations with Philip we began to uncover the significance of Philip's resilience. The following questions provided a context for these conversations.

- *Given you have told me how you experienced virtually no control of your life when you had to share the same room as your brother, was playing racing cars an area of your life where you experienced control?*

- *From playing this game and experiencing a sense of control over your own life, what message did this give you about hope for the future?*

- *Did this make it more or less possible to feel safe? Why?*

- *Did it take imagination to play racing cars?*

- *Does this discovery and appreciation of imagination stand against your brother's questioning of your intelligence?*

Gradually a story of resilience became more available to Philip.

4. Stories of connection

Many men who have been subject to abuse describe experiencing a sense of profound isolation. As men tell their story, however, exceptions to this isolation are often revealed. Stories of connection to other people in the past and present can work against a problem-saturated story of disconnection to others. In some cases men begin to confront self-blame by acknowledging the significance of various positive relationships they have built with others.

Chad, for example, had experienced disempowerment and self-blame as a result of being raped by a family friend when he was thirteen years old. The perpetrator was charged and convicted. Following this, Chad's family remained silent about the abuse and encouraged him to forget about the assault. Chad began to experience a general sense of 'not fitting in' with other people. He blamed himself and felt his experience of abuse was known to others by the way he looked and acted. Due to the influence of self-blame, Chad believed people saw him as inferior.

As we explored Chad's experience he recalled a teacher who had noticed his skills in creative writing. The teacher had given him encouragement to use his 'flair' and this had been an experience that stood outside of the reign of self-blame. Following this re-discovery Chad began to recognise friends that had stood against negative self-talk. He recalled being unsuccessful at exams and how he and a small group of friends (who had also been unsuccessful at exams) had joined in mateship. He spoke of how this had helped to challenge the negative influences of self-blame. Some questions helped this process:

- *I understand that at school you felt 'doomed to fail', yet despite this you have remembered your teacher's recognition of your 'flair' and her encouragement. What do you put this down to?*
- *What do you think she saw in you that she wanted to encourage?*
- *Would this remembering be an action that stands against feeling a failure?*
- *Did your connection with your mates around the problem with exams have you feeling more or less different?*
- *What might it tell you about yourself that others may have seen you as a mate?*

Acknowledging acts of protest, resistance, resilience and connection in the present

These stories of protest, resistance, resilience and connection are often supported by actions that the men are taking in their lives in the present. Yet self-blame can attempt to recruit the men into seeing these actions are negative or 'maladaptive'. Some of the men who I have consulted with have demonstrated significant protest when they have feared that others may be vulnerable to the actions of the person who perpetrated abuse against them.

Imran, for example, had never disclosed to anyone about being sexually abused by his uncle. His experience of being silenced had been significant in his younger years. This changed for Imran as an adult man when he heard that his uncle was facing criminal charges and had enlisted the support of Imran's parents to defend the charges. This caused substantial distress for Imran. Knowing the effects of not being believed, he quickly decided to speak out to support his nieces.

This action in the present stood alongside Imran's actions of protest as a child when he refused to be left in the company of his uncle. We traced this connection in our conversations.

Imran spoke out telling his parents, aunty and partner of the abuse he had been subjected to, and he offered statements to the police and welfare authorities. This was a difficult process as people began to question Imran as to why he had not disclosed his abuse as a child. Despite many invitations to question his experience of being silenced as a child and to blame himself, Imran was able to hold onto his experience of himself as a young man who had stood against abuse. The stories of protest and resilience that he had developed in relation to his earlier experiences held firmly under great stress.

Imran was able to show his strength as an adult to speak up for young children. We explored what this meant for Imran. Imran was also able to take further steps against self-blame through his connection with his nieces. He came to identify more clearly the predatory nature of his uncle's abuse. He came to see that his uncle had not differentiated between children but that his abuse was opportunistic.

Those who were aligned to his uncle's denial of the abuse initially dismissed Imran's disclosure - stating that is was fuelled by a 'vendetta'. Yet Imran persisted in speaking out and was supported by his sister who had also experienced abuse from the same uncle. The uncle's partner at this stage began to take Imran and his sister seriously and the support for his uncle's denial was withdrawn.

Tracing the links between Imran's earlier actions of resilience and protest with these current stories of resistance and connection - with his nieces and his sister - enabled Imran to become clearer about what he had always stood for in his life. In this way, actions of protest in the present provided rich opportunity for the re-storying of Imran's life away from stories of isolation and self-blame and towards stories of connection and justice.

Talking about physiological responses

Self-blame is often associated with the physiological responses that some men experience during sexual abuse. Self-blame is quick to construct the meaning that a physiological response is a sign of consent. Many men experience great confusion in relation to this issue, particularly as in many cases the victim's physiological response has been used by the perpetrator to justify his actions.

Finding non-confronting ways to speak about this issue can be challenging. Speaking about the experiences of other men who have experienced abuse can perhaps make the conversations easier. I often name that other men I have spoken to have experienced an erection or ejaculation during abuse, while taking care to acknowledge that this may or may not be the experience of the man I am speaking with. Offering information about physiological responses is another alternative. Practical information about how if the penis is touched in certain ways it will react, and how if the prostrate is pressured from the wall of the anus it can cause ejaculation, can assist the process of liberation from self-blame. Citing evidence of how these physiological responses are involuntary actions that in no way imply consent or desire seems important. Lew (1993) and Hunter (1990) have both documented that physiological response during sexual abuse is a common experience of male victims of sexual abuse. I have found these references helpful to assist in dis-empowering self-blame.

Challenging pathological notions of disorder or damage

Many of the men and young men with whom I have consulted in relation to childhood sexual abuse have been subject to psychological and/or psychiatric assessments which have at times contributed to notions of a 'damaged identity'. In some circumstances the way in which psychiatric or psychological labels are applied to men who have experienced abuse can inadvertently encourage self-blame, silencing, powerlessness and guilt. Pathological notions of damage can situate the effects of abuse as beyond the person's power. They can imply that the effects of abuse are now characteristic of the person's identity. This can have significant implications for the avenues open to men to resolve the problems they are experiencing and their ability to take personal responsibility.

Finding ways to acknowledge the man's understanding of the origin of the mental health issue he may be facing can be a liberating process. Similarly for those who have been recruited into believing that they are 'going crazy', tracing the reasons for this 'craziness' can be a grounding experience and one that brings substantial relief. For some men, making the link between their experience of depression and their experience of abuse has changed the meaning of psychiatric treatment and has been a precursor to finding their own healing ways.

George, for example, when referred to a psychiatric casualty department because of serious concerns about his suicidal thinking, made it clear how important it was to him that the connection between his state of mind and the abuse he experienced was acknowledged. As I waited with him to be admitted he consistently asked, 'Do they know why I am here?' and 'Do they know what happened?' in a way that was clearly making a statement about the abuse and where responsibility lay for his state of mind. In our conversations and our liaison with psychiatric staff, George's experience of depression and self-hate were clearly attributed to his experience of being subjected to childhood sexual abuse. George said that this attribution made it more possible for him to regain clarity and power over his own life.

Dimitri's story provides another example. Dimitri has a significant history of contact with the mental health system. The following extract comes from a conversation in which we celebrated some of the steps he has taken in dealing with his experience of childhood sexual abuse and the increased independence he has gained from the mental health system.

Patrick: *That's something we have talked about, how feeling crazy was connected to a lot of the effects of abuse we wrote on the board that time.*

Dimitri: *Yeah.*

Patrick: *And that there hasn't been much room given by the mental health system to talk about the effects of the abuse.*

Dimitri: *Yeah, about ten years of it and the doctors didn't say anything about it.*

Patrick: *How do you think they failed to hear about your experience of the problem?*

Dimitri: *The system just took me under its wing, but didn't recognise what had happened. They sort of took power away in a lot of ways.*

Patrick: *There have been some pretty big moves for you in asking to move away from the group home. Is that a stand you have made about having more power in decisions about your life?*

Dimitri: *Yeah.*

Patrick: *How have you done this?*

Dimitri: *Through not having to go to hospital so much and getting my own place, I can do more of my own thing without them knowing.*

Pathological understandings of the effects of abuse serve to silence the history of these effects and fail to locate responsibility for these effects with the abuse and the abuser. Finding ways to trace the history and responsibility can be a liberating process.

Pathological understandings of the effects of abuse can also inadvertently increase a man's sense of powerlessness over his own life and actions. In my experience of consulting with young men who have been subjected to abuse, a significant proportion have been given a diagnosis of disorders such as ADHD (Attention Deficit Hyperactive Disorder) and Conduct Disorder. These diagnoses can have implications for the young man's development and also for his relationships with significant others. Max, for example, reported that, 'I can just about get away with anything at home because of the abuse and what the doctor said about having ADD'. Max felt absolved from any sense of responsibility to find ways to protest the effects of abuse or other problems in his life. The diagnosis constructed his life and identity as problematic. In this way Max was left in a position in which the significant people in his life had pathological understandings of his actions, and his identity. This had implications for his behaviour and his attribution of personal responsibility for his future. The need to find ways of inviting men who have experienced abuse to feel an increased sense of personal agency and with it an increased responsibility for their actions is discussed below.

Deconstructing interactional notions of entrapment in an abuse cycle

As discussed earlier, it is common within the media, within service delivery, policy and individual practice, for links to be made in relation to males being subjected to abuse and going on to perpetrate abuse. It is not uncommon for men to express concern that because they experienced child sexual abuse they may have a predisposition to also act in sexually abusive ways. When men express this concern I am interested in addressing three areas. Firstly, to establish whether or not they have ever acted in a sexually abusive ways. Secondly, to explore how they have come to this concern of theirs in relation to the propensity to abuse. Thirdly, to invite them to be clear about their position in relation to being for or against sexually abusive behaviour, and to explore the meanings of such a stand in their life. Various questions facilitate explorations in these areas.

- *Have you ever been concerned that you would ever behave in a sexually abusive way?*
- *Are you worried you may have acted in ways that are sexually abusive?*
- *Would naming your concerns be a stand against sexual abuse?*
- *Is this what you want?*
- *Is one of the effects of abuse to encourage you to think you could become sexually abusive yourself? Why?*
- *Is this a position aligned to self-blame?*
- *Given you have expressed concern to me about the thought of becoming sexually abusive, what does this say about what you are wanting for your life?*
- *Would naming your concern make it more or less likely for you to act abusively?*
- *Why do you suppose people who have experienced abuse believe they might go on to abuse?*

Creating space within therapeutic conversations for men to speak of their concerns in relation to acting abusively to others seems very important. In circumstances where the man has had concerns about the chance of him abusing others because of his sexual victimisation, it is an opportunity to invite the man to see these concerns as a continuation of his stand against the effects of sexual abuse. It is an opportunity to make a clear distinction between having thoughts of abusing to actually abusing other people. It is an opportunity to invite the man to take a position in relation to the power of choice. It is possible to make clearer the distinction between being subject to abuse and subjecting others to abuse.

When a man does disclose that he has been responsible for sexually abusive actions, this then provides a starting-point to address these issues. In most situations I then refer these men to specialised counsellors who can work conjointly on the issue of being subjected to sexual abuse and later acting abusively. While being clear to in no way diminish the effects that the man's sexually abusive actions may have had on others, nor to deny in any way his responsibility for those actions, it is sometimes possible to situate the man's disclosure of abusive actions as an indication of his intentions not to act abusively. This can begin a process of talking about steps of redress and steps necessary to prevent further harm.

Within these conversations I am careful not to assume that the man has had thoughts he could sexually abuse others. I am careful to speak in ways that do not imply that he has or has not acted in sexually abusive ways.

These sorts of conversations are especially relevant in situations in which men speak of how abuse has occurred to a significant proportion of family members across generations. Deconstructing understandings of the inevitability of abuse, or the cycle of victim to perpetrator, can enable men to be explicit about their own sense of self-power and responsibility. It also creates more room for the man's identity to be based on alterative ways of being a man, ways based on respect and care.

Standing against the reproduction of male violence

Like myself, the males I consult with live within dominant men's culture. As a result, many of them may be involved in practices that are subjugating of others. Some men may be involved in acts of violence, while others may have an exaggerated sense of entitlement in their relationships with others. Finding ways to invite men who been subjected to abuse to take steps towards developing a congruency in their positions against violence and abuse is an important part of this work.

Often a central issue for the men who consult with me is their experience of anger in relation to the abuse they experienced as a child. The ways in which this anger is understood makes a significant difference to its consequences. This anger can be understood as legitimate rage in response to violent actions. Within the dominant ideas of masculinity, however, experiences of anger and rage are all too often seen as connected to, and as justifying of, violent and aggressive acts - acts that replicate the worst of masculine culture. Acknowledging injustice and the rightful response of rage seems important. Expressions of anger are understandable and often act as catalysts for seeking redress and for stepping outside of notions of self-blame. However, when expressions of anger replicate abuse and are aligned with dominant forms of oppressive masculinity, they are often counter-productive not only for the man himself but for those around him.

Inviting men to speak of their histories of protest against violence and abuse creates a context in which they can take a stand against all forms of abusive actions. Through exploring these men's experiences of abuse, stories of standing against abuse are often articulated in great detail. Philip, for example, began to understand his actions as developing a 'personal loyalty' *against* abuse and *for* alternative ways of being a man. The stories of protest against the abuse he was subjected to came to represent for him a stand against dominant men's ways of being in the world. They began to be seen as congruent with a stand against all forms of violence and control.

The following questions informed our conversations:

- *In relation to the stories that we have shared together, of the ways you resisted the effects of abuse, do these stories paint a picture of you being pro-violence or against violence?*

- *Who would be the least surprised that you are determined to find non-violent ways of being?*

- *What stories would they share about you if they were here?*

- *In facing up to the ways in which your partner experiences some of your behaviour as controlling, is this a further step in standing against violence?*

- *In acknowledging those times when you have replicated violence or felt like replicating violence, what does this say about the life you wish to lead?*

When talking about the issue of anger, the following questions have been a useful guide:

- *What are some of the different sorts of anger? What can they lead to?*

- *As men, what are we taught about ways of expressing anger?*

- *When you talked about your anger at the abuse you were subjected to, was this anger a statement of belief that you deserved to be treated respectfully?*

- *Are there other times when you experience an anger that stands up for respectful ways of being?*

- *What does this sort of anger look like?*

- *What sort of actions does it lead to?*

- *Are there times when you experience different sorts of anger? An anger that can lead to disrespectful ways?*

- *What are some ways that this anger could be expressed that would fit with your preferred ways of being?*

Men have mentioned various ways of expressing anger that do not replicate violence or abuse including: writing letters of testimony; writing letters to the people who were responsible for the abuse; and inviting significant persons to therapy sessions to honour the man's experiences of injustice and the ways he has got through them.

These conversations about men's violence and anger aim to enable men to take a stand, not only against the abuse they have been subject to, but also against abuse and violence more generally. These conversations seek to clarify the sorts of lives that the men wish to lead. Appreciating their own histories of resisting violent ways of being often clarifies and builds upon what they want for their lives. The conversations contribute to living lives based on non-violent ways of being.

Acknowledgement and testimony of preferred ways of being

During the therapeutic journey there are often opportunities to acknowledge and celebrate the terrain that has been traversed and all that has been accomplished. Finding ways of confirming alternative stories of survival and resilience, as well as stories of alternative ways of being men, is a continual process. For some men, formalising what has occurred in their lives, the changes they have made, feels important. During the final stages of consulting together we often create a document of identity which details the journey the man has taken. Holding a ceremony and inviting significant others to attend and reflect upon the changes that have occurred can be powerfully acknowledging. In some circumstances it is preferred that I document some of our important conversations in the form of a letter which can then serve as a testimony to the man's work.

My experience of this work

Being witness to stories of abuse and sorrow, of powerlessness and grief, and being witness to stories of protest, resilience and self-care, I experience as a privilege. Speaking with other men as they separate themselves from the effects of the worst extremes of masculine culture and seek to create for themselves new, alternative ways of being men, offers me, as a man, a sense of hopefulness. It offers me a sense that as men we can build upon alternative ways of relating and begin to redress the harm caused by masculine ways of being to women, children and ourselves.

Central to this sense of hopefulness are processes of accountability. As discussed throughout this paper, working with males who have been subjected to abuse occurs within a broader context of adult power over children, professional's power over those who consult with them, men's violence and inequitable gender relations. Finding ways to consistently name that I may unwittingly reproduce oppressive practices, and finding ways to ensure that I am working in ways that are transparent and accountable to those who are consulting me as well as to women workers in the field, enables me to find hope, sustenance and joy in this work.

Acknowledgements

The information presented in this paper has evolved from a history of support from, and partnership with, a significant number of people. I was introduced to ways of understanding the dynamics of abuse while working with men who use violence against their women partners. Dallas Colley, Lesley Porter and Rob Hall were influential in introducing me to ways of working that prioritise accountability, acknowledge the political nature of the work, and seek to be respectful of all who are involved. Three years ago, when I began to work at Adelaide Central Mission, I was encouraged by Maxine Joy to consult with male survivors of childhood sexual abuse. Maxine's work and the conversations we have shared have invited me to more fully appreciate the position and experience of children in relation to sexual abuse. Her generosity of ideas, support and supervision have contributed significantly to the work described in this paper. Over the last three years my employer, the Adelaide Central Mission, has offered unreserved support for developing a counselling service for males who have experienced childhood sexual abuse. This has occurred in a spirit of partnership between male and female workers. I have also been encouraged by Jim Barber at Flinders University to be creative, and I have been supported to develop knowledge in this area and to write about this work by both Adelaide Central Mission and Flinders University. In the process of writing up this work, David Denborough played a significant role as editor and became a valued and loved friend in re-working sections of the text, as well as interviewing me and helping me connect with my experiences of this work.

I also must find space to say that persisting to get this paper completed and finding a way forward through some tough moments has been my own little 'Everest'. I would like to thank those people who supported me. I would especially like to thank Lester Rigney for his passionate pep talk that reignited my determination to write about this issue.

Finally, it is important to acknowledge that it is due to the courage and trust of those men and young men with whom I have consulted that this paper has been written. The work described has evolved through our conversations and the therapeutic relationships that we have built together.

Notes

1. First published in the 1998 No.4 *Dulwich Centre Journal.* Republished here with permission.

    This paper is to provide the basis for a detailed practice write-up to be produced by the Adelaide Central Mission.

2. Patrick O'Leary is currently undertaking PhD studies at Flinders University of South Australia and is working as a counsellor in a part-time capacity at the Adelaide Central Mission.

    He can be contacted c/- Dulwich Centre Publications, Hutt St PO Box 7192, Adelaide 5000, South Australia, or on email: SAPJOL@sigma.sss.flinders.edu.au

3. See Finkelhor 1986.

4. See Holmes, Offen & Waller 1997; Dhaliwal, Gauzas, Antonowicz & Ross 1996; Dorais 1997; Mendel 1995; Urquiza & Capra 1990.

5. See Farrell 1994.

6. A recent review of North American studies has revealed that approximately 30% of all childhood sexual abuse victims are male (Holmes, Offen & Waller 1997).

7. See Kamsler 1990; Kazan 1994.

8. See Connell 1995; Denborough 1996; McLean, Carey & White 1996.

9. See Connell 1995.

10. Hansen and Slater (1988, cited in Romano & DeLuca 1997) studied literature and found an average of 28 % of sex offenders had experienced child sexual abuse, whilst Bagley (1994, cited in Romano & DeLuca 1997) found a figure of 15.5%. More recently Ryan et al. (1996) found that 39.1% of child molesters had experienced child sexual assault. Locally in South Australia the Adolescent Sexual Abuse Prevention Program (1996, cited Hall & O'Leary 1997) found that 37% of adolescent sex offenders had been abused as children.

11. I was introduced to the ideas within this section by Maxine Joy.

References

Alcoff, L. & Gray, L. 1993: 'Survivor discourse: Transgression or recuperation?' *Signs,* Winter, pp.260-290.

Connell, R.W. 1995: *Masculinities.* NSW, Australia: Allen & Unwin.

Denborough, D. 1996: *Beyond the Prison: Gathering dreams of freedom.* Adelaide: Dulwich Centre Publications.

Dhaliwal, G.K., Gauzas, L., Antonowicz, D.H. & Ross, R.R. 1996: 'Adult male survivors of childhood sexual abuse: Prevalence, sexual abuse characteristics, and long-term effects.' *Clinical Psychology Review,* 16(7):616-639. Pergamon Press. USA.

Farrell, W. 1994: *The Myth of Male Power: Why men are the disposable sex.* New York: Simon & Schuster.

Finkelhor, D. 1984: *Child Sexual Abuse.* New York: The Free Press.

Finkelhor, D. 1986: *A Sourcebook on Child Sexual Abuse*. California: Sage Publications.

Finkelhor, D. & Browne, A. 1985: 'The traumatic impact of child sexual abuse: A conceptualization.' *American Journal of Orthopsychiatric Association*, 55(4).

Freud, S. (1900) 1953: *The Interpretation of Dreams. Complete psychological works*. Standard Edition. Vol.4-5. London: Hogarth.

Hall, R. & O'Leary, P.J. 1997: 'Abuse and the construction of identity in young men and adolescent boys.' Conference Paper presented at the *Second National Men's Health Conference*, Fremantle, Western Australia.

Homes, G.R., Offen, L. & Walker, G. 1997: 'See no evil, hear no evil, speak no evil: Why do relatively few male victims of childhood sexual abuse receive help for abuse - Related issues in adulthood.' *Clinical Psychology Review*, 17(1):69-88. Pergamon Press.

Hunter, M. (ed) 1990: *The Sexually Abused Male: Prevalence, impact and treatment*, Vol.1&2. USA: Lexington Books.

Kamsler, A. 1990: 'Her-story in the making: Therapy with women who were sexually abused in childhood.' In Durrant, M. & White, C. (eds), *Ideas for Therapy with Sexual Abuse*. Adelaide: Dulwich Centre Publications.

Kazan, Z. 1994: 'Power: A multi-dimensional perspective.' *Dulwich Centre Newsletter*, No.1.

Lew, M. 1993: *Victims No Longer: A guide for men recovering from sexual child abuse*. USA: Cedar.

McLean, C., Carey, M. & White, C. (eds) 1996: *Men's Ways of Being*. Colorado: Westview Press.

Mendel, M.P. 1993: 'Issues of particular salience to male survivors of childhood sexual abuse.' *Family Violence and Sexual Assault Bulletin*, 9(1).

Mendel, M.P. 1995: *The Male Survivor: The impact of sexual abuse*. London: Sage.

Nasjleti, M. 1980: 'Suffering in silence: The male incest victim.' *Child Welfare*, Vol.LIX, No.5, May. USA: Child Welfare League of America.

Romano, E. & DeLuca, R.V. 1997: 'Exploring the relationship between childhood sexual abuse and adult sexual perpetration.' *Journal of Family Violence*, 12(1).

Ryan, G., Miyoshi, T.J., Metzner, J.L., Krugman, R.D. & Fryer, G.E. 1996: 'Trends in a national sample of sexually abusive youths.' *Journal of the American Academy of Child and Adolescent Psychiatry*, 35(1).

White, M. 1994: *Re-Authoring Lives: Interviews & essays*. Adelaide: Dulwich Centre Publications.

PART VI

New Ways of
Introducing
Narrative Therapy

13

The one-minute question: What is narrative therapy?

Some working answers [1]

by

Erik Sween [2]

It is a familiar scenario. Some well meaning person asks, 'What is narrative therapy?', and then glances at her/his watch to indicate s/he only has time for a short answer. It is a dilemma I think every narrative therapist has faced. Each time it happens I want to cringe. What should I say? I search for the right words, scan the memory banks, and try my best. But I rarely feel my answer communicates any adequate representation of narrative ideas. Too often my response has drawn a polite nod and an awkward silence. Somehow I want to find a way to share some of my interest and enthusiasm about narrative therapy with the people who ask me the question.

Perhaps there is no answer to the one-minute question. At the same time, I am not comfortable dodging the question. Although I have used this strategy more than I like to admit, somehow, in my discomfort, I like the question. It poses a challenge. Can I explain what I do in public language? Can I use words that can be understood by non-experts? Of course, it is easier to communicate with narrative colleagues because of the common language and world-view we share. But that involves a 'preaching to the choir'. Another aspect of the challenge comes from my belief in the power of narrative therapy. I feel these ideas have something valuable to offer people who are unfamiliar with them. In that way, I do not want to be part of turning people away from the ideas. Some of them may eventually be as grateful as I have been for understanding narrative concepts.

So, here are my best attempts at responding to the one-minute question. Each response is intended to stand on its own. Multiple answers are provided for different days of the week or for different audiences - whichever proves more useful. Order is arbitrary and not meant to signify importance.

1. If narrative therapy had one slogan, it would be: 'The person is never the problem; the problem is the problem'. This phrase captures the importance attached to who a person is, regardless of his or her circumstances. Narrative therapy involves exploring the shaping moments of a person's life, the turning-points, the key relationships, and those particular memories not dimmed by time. Focus is drawn to the intentions, dreams, and values that have guided a person's life, despite the set-backs. Oftentimes, the process brings back stories that have been overlooked - surprising stories that speak of forgotten competence and heroism.

2. Every type of psychotherapy designates a different aspect of life as the basic unit of experience. For example, behavioural therapy focuses on behaviour, cognitive therapy focuses on logical thinking, while systems therapy focuses on family interaction as the basic unit. In this way, narrative therapy holds up the story as the basic unit of experience. Stories guide how people act, think, feel, and make sense of new experience. Stories organise the information from a person's life. Narrative therapy focuses on how these important stories can get written and rewritten.

3. Narrative therapy proposes that people use certain stories about themselves like the lens on a camera. These stories have the effect of filtering a person's experience and thereby selecting what information gets focused in or focused out. These stories shape people's perspectives of their lives, histories, and

futures. Despite information to the contrary, these stories of identity can be remarkably stable. Narrative therapy provides a means to refocus the lens on this camera and help reshape a person's stories and life.

4. As people, we are inescapably meaning-makers. We have an experience and then attach meaning to it. Since time immemorial, and the days around the campfire, we have been telling stories. Stories are our most familiar means of communicating the meaning we find in our experiences. Narrative therapy is interested in the stories we live by - those stories we carry with us about who we are and what is most important to us. Narrative therapy involves unearthing these stories, understanding them, and re-telling them.

5. Many forms of psychology and therapy place enormous emphasis on the process of individuation. In this way, the individual is believed to construct her or his internal world almost single-handedly. Narrative therapy provides a contrast to this perspective. Narrative therapy proposes that identity is co-created in relationship with other people as well as by one's history and culture. Thus, being seen by others in a certain way can contribute as much as seeing oneself in a certain way. We come to see ourselves by looking in the mirrors that other people hold up for us. In this way, a person's identity is said to be socially constructed. Narrative therapy focuses on the degree to which that socially constructed identity fits for that person.

6. Narrative therapy consists of understanding the stories or themes that have shaped a person's life. Out of all the experiences a person has lived, what has held the most meaning? What choices, intentions, relationships have been most important? Narrative therapy proposes that only those experiences that are part of a larger story will have significant impact on a person's lived experience. Therefore, narrative therapy focuses on building the plot which connects a person's life together.

7. A person's life is criss-crossed by invisible story-lines. These unseen story-lines can have enormous power in shaping a person's life. Narrative therapy involves the process of drawing out and amplifying these story-lines. Questions are used to focus on what has been most meaningful in a person's

life. Common areas of inquiry include intentions, influential relationships, turning-points, treasured memories, and how these areas connect with each other.

8. ...

Obviously, this list could keep going. But these are my current working answers. The last number is left blank to indicate a 'work in progress' as well as the multiplicity of possible answers. While I am not searching for a definitive answer or one that will appeal to everyone, I feel the question keeps me on a creative edge. It keeps me trying to articulate these ideas without using jargon and trying to communicate with people outside of the narrative therapy community. It also reminds me of the words of my dissertation adviser from long ago: 'If you can't explain the idea in three sentences to your grandmother, the idea is not clear enough in your own mind'.

Notes

1. First published in the 1998 Vol.2 *Gecko*. Republished here with permission.
2. Erik can be contacted c/- 767 Pearl St, Suite 220, Boulder, Colorado, USA, email: erik@boulder.net

14

Practice Notes:
Introducing narrative ways of working[1]

by

Alice Morgan[2]

How do I introduce narrative ways of working to a group of students who are embarking on a two-year training course? This question occupied my thoughts recently as I prepared a two and a half day workshop for a group of thirty-eight people enrolled in their first year of a two-year training course in narrative therapy at Dulwich Centre in Adelaide, South Australia.

The following pages describe an exercise I conducted with the group and some of my thoughts. I will also share some of the participants' responses to the activity and explore how they have contributed to an ongoing deconstruction of some educational practices which I am interested in challenging.

Hopes for the exercise

My major interest was to find ways of explaining that narrative ways of working constitute more than a series of techniques. I was looking for a way to demonstrate some of the key beliefs, values and interests that inform narrative therapy. I hoped that this would mean that discussions about various narrative practices, for example externalising conversations, would be situated within a context of broader beliefs, ideas and principles. I very much wanted to invite respectful ways of relating within the group; to demonstrate an interest in each student; and to acknowledge the unique skills and knowledges that each student would be bringing to the course. The following exercise was an attempt to address these sorts of issues.

The exercise involved giving the group members the choice of filling in two very different questionnaires. The two forms, which were hypothetical, contained some questions that I presumed would be fairly familiar to the group from a range of different contexts, as well as some that may have been new to the group. For me, an important aspect of narrative is interacting with people through questions. I hoped that these questionnaires would give an immediate experience of different ways of asking questions and their potential effects.

Introducing the exercise

I explained that we would begin the workshop with an exercise that I hoped would be thought-provoking in relation to narrative ways of working and that would offer some sense of the work. My directions went something like this:

In a moment I'm going to give you two forms - one is printed on white paper (Form A) and the other is printed on a variety of coloured pieces of paper (Form B). I'll pass them around and would like you to take one of each. Please choose a colour that you like from the Form B pile and then read through the questions. They are two very different forms and I'm going to ask you to choose the one which you would prefer to fill in. Before you choose, however, I'll explain some of the 'rules' for each form. I'd like you to select the form that you'd prefer to fill in.

[As an aside] Before I do that, can I just say now that there are no tricks to this exercise and that my thinking behind giving it to you is for you to begin to explore the questions that are on each form. I won't be asking you for your answers. After the exercise we will be talking about the differences in the questions, not your individual answers.

I wanted to be transparent about the purpose of the exercise from its outset. I was aware that being assessed or judged by 'the teacher' could have been a common (negative) experience for some of the participants in their past learning contexts and I wanted to make sure that I did not reproduce any of these practices.

I continued with the instructions and made notes on the whiteboard as I spoke.

If you choose Form A: these are the following guidelines. You will have 25 minutes to complete the form. Please remain in this room, in your seat and answer the questions in order. Please use a pen. I will collect the papers at the end of the 25 minutes. I will remain in the room while you complete the form.

For people who prefer Form B: I've allowed 25 minutes for this but will come and check with you to see how you're going and whether you need more or less time to do it. Feel free to go anywhere you like - the park, coffee shop, outside, by the fountain, in the kitchen, wherever you feel comfortable (if you leave the building perhaps you could check back with me after 25 minutes and we'll negotiate from there!) Answer any of the questions that interest you - you might like to answer all of them, some, just one, or even none of them. That's fine. At the front of the room are all sorts of things that you might like to use - coloured pens, crayons, pencils, lots of different sized pieces of papers, scissors, and glue. If you'd like anything else, just let me know and I'll see what I can do. You can be as creative as you like - poetry, writing, drawing, painting, whatever takes your fancy. The information in response to the questions is yours, and it is up to you if you wish to share any of your responses and with whom.

Just let me say again, that at the end of the exercise we will get together to discuss the types of questions and some of the differences that you noticed, not the content of your answers.

The forms that I handed out are included over the page.

Form A: Instructions[3]

You will have 25 minutes to complete this questionnaire. Please answer questions in order and give as much information as possible in the spaces provided.

Name: Mr, Mrs, Miss, Ms:

                                               Title (if applicable):

Address:

Marital Status:

Number of Children:

List your academic qualifications in order from highest to lowest:

Past work experience:

Current place of employment:

In the past have you suffered from any of the following (please tick):
         depression   anxiety
         family break-up   stress
         heart condition   poor physical or mental health
         obsessive compulsive disorder   schizophrenia
         eating problems   trauma
         Other (please specify)

Name of 2 Referees:

Address:

Occupation & Position:

For Office Use only

```
┌─────────────────────┐
│                     │
│                     │
│                     │
└─────────────────────┘
```

Form B: Optional Questionnaire

Reflect on some of the following questions and answer those that interest you. 25 minutes has been allowed for this exercise, however Alice will consult the group at the end of that time to negotiate if more time is needed. The questionnaire belongs to you - all information is confidential and it is up to you who you share it with. At the end of the time we will discuss what the questions were like to answer (not the content of your answers).

At the front of the room there is more paper and other bits of equipment that you may like to use. Please don't feel confined to use the spaces provided below - put as much/little detail in your reflections as suits you.

What name do you like to be called? What do you like about that?

Is there a place that holds precious memories for you? What makes this place special for you?

During your life what learnings or knowledges have been positive for you? What contribution have they made to your life?

In your life, what experiences and knowledges do you value?

Think about someone (person or animal) in your life (alive or no longer living) that is particularly important to you and knows about your special skills. How would this person describe you? What skills, abilities, qualities, values would they talk about? What would they say if they were asked, 'What personal qualities/strengths stand out to you about X that will contribute to this course?' How would you respond to this? Would you add any to the ones they would talk about?

How have you managed to overcome difficulties in the past? What personal strengths and abilities did you draw upon? What did it take for you to do this? How do your experiences contribute positively to the lives of those who consult you?

Is there anyone you would like to share these reflections with? Why? What contribution would sharing this have on their life and on your life?

What do you think about these questions and doing this task? What has been interesting to you? What would you like to think more about?

Members of the group selected their preferred form and began. After 25 minutes I asked any of the people in the room who were completing Form A to hand their papers to me. I found those completing Form B and tentatively asked them how they were going. Do you need more time? Would you be ready to join the big group yet? How much longer would you like, etc.? As it happened, only one person chose to complete Form A. He explained afterwards that he had filled in so many forms in his life that he just did not have the energy for forms at all, and Form A was easier. This in itself is a clear example of how such forms can close down space and prevent the exploration of new possibilities.

Discussion

When we assembled again as a large group I asked: 'Would anyone like to comment on what they noticed about the differences between the two forms?' I had prepared a lot of questions previously that I thought I might draw upon but found that I didn't use many of them as the group quickly and spontaneously offered their ideas. I wrote up their responses on the whiteboard in two columns headed Form A and Form B.

You may be interested in some of the questions I had prepared in advance:

- *What types of knowledges were the forms interested in?*
- *What was the overall tone of the questions?*
- *Who held the expertise?*
- *Did you notice any differences in the power relationships between the administrator and you?*
- *How were difficulties/problems thought about?*
- *How were issues of gender, class, culture, sexual preference and age addressed?*
- *How were other people referred to? In what context and on what basis were they consulted?*
- *What information were they asked to offer?*
- *Who 'owned' the information?*

- *What would be the real effects on you as a person after completing them?*
- *How would a person be 'left' after doing them?*
- *What options for comment and evaluation were given?*
- *What particular ideas shaped the questions? For example, questions about age, academic qualifications, address, etc.*

Lively discussion followed.[4] We ended up with a rich and vivid description of some of the values and ethics of narrative work under the column marked Form B, and comments and words under the column marked Form A.

People spoke about how honouring Form B was, the respect they noticed in the questions, how the questions were hopeful for the future, and acknowledged individual strengths, abilities and competencies. Many of them spoke about what they noticed about the types of knowledges that were valued in each form: Form A honouring academic, 'formal' institutional knowledges, the honouring of other people's knowledges (with formal qualifications and positions) above personal knowledge. The group commented that the spaces provided for each answer in Form A indicated the preference for 'formal training' over 'work experience'.[3] They discussed how Form B honoured many types of knowledges and highlighted the contribution of lived experience. 'We were the experts about our own life - the experts weren't the people reading the form.' The heterosexual dominance of the language in Form A was quickly articulated, as was the implications of the box marked 'For Office Use only'.

The group spoke about how problems were talked about. In Form A many were concerned about the pathologising language, the labelling. They asked, 'How do you define terms like depression, stress, anxiety? Who has the right to define them?' I asked them what they understood to be the purpose of asking questions about 'problems' which they had experienced in their lives. The group wondered if the purpose was to categorise participants along a continuum of ideas around 'normalcy'. We discussed the implications of the responses - was it to ensure that these issues were 'dealt' with before people embarked on any therapy with other people, as they would be seen to get in the way of the therapeutic relationship? Or was it assuming that these problems revealed something about the 'essential' identity of the person, as being a part of them which would be always present, that is, once a depressive, always a depressive?

Many of the group commented about how refreshed they felt at the way in which problems were referred to in Form B. Some people appreciated the assumptions inherent in the language of the questions that implicitly recognised the existence of people's strengths and abilities. They also commented on how the questions assumed that people are able to overcome difficulties. They noted that Form B appreciated people's contribution to reducing the effects of problems in their lives; that is, they recognised the existence of personal agency.

Many were surprised at one of the questions: 'How do your experiences contribute positively to the lives of those who consult you?' Some said they had never considered this. They commented on how Form A presumed that a therapist's personal experience of problems would interfere with being a 'good therapist' rather than making a positive contribution. Some of the group members spoke of their interest in thinking more about the questions on Form B and predicted this further thinking would contribute positively to their work and life.

Some of their other comments were as follows:

- *With Form B you would find out so many things about the person, there was so much scope for individuality. There is space for the expression of people's personalities, skills and passions.*

- *Form B had me thinking so many different things - thoughts I've never had before - and helped me to remember some precious things about my life.*

- *Form B had measures of accountability and evaluation and room for people to say what they thought about the questions.*

- *The questions on Form B fitted with Aboriginal ways. When I read them I thought 'Yeah, this fits with my people'.*

Standing at the front of the room as an audience to these reflections and as a scribe for the group, I felt rather overwhelmed at just how easily we were articulating some of the 'principles of narrative' and how they were offering them so spontaneously. I was reflecting on how, in my own learning, this had taken me a long time to articulate and I was rejoicing at how easily the group were doing this. What was important for me was that an appreciation of the richness of narrative work, as more than a technique, was being clearly expressed. I noticed when they were discussing Form B that there was a spirit of excitement and curiosity in the group - a sense of fun and collaboration.

I was somewhat surprised at just how easy it was for the group to grasp the concept that questions are informed by particular ways of thinking, and to identify these ways of thinking in this exercise. I consider this to be very important in embarking on a study of this work. I have found that being free of the idea that 'narrative is about asking questions' and 'I just have to ask the right question' is very helpful. I find that once I am familiar with narrative ways of thinking, the questions flow easily from that foundation. In conversations with the people who consult me, I am more free to explore a range of possibilities with them, and questions flow more naturally. The experience of the conversation tends to be more enriching for all involved.

I anticipated some of the group's answers but was really pleased to hear many things that I had not anticipated. In particular, I had underestimated the effect of Form B on the personal lives of the people completing it. When planning it, I was confident that the group would find the questions interesting, different and honouring of them. I wanted it to bring attention to some of the dominant discourses of education and 'educational knowledge', and hoped it would contribute to challenging notions of the 'expert' and the power differential between 'teacher' and 'student' inherent in these discourses and their practices. I did not, however, predict the contribution the questions on Form B would make to their thoughts and feelings about beginning the course. This became clear when we discussed the possible effects on people's lives of completing each form. The group discussed how Form A would leave someone feeling incompetent, problem-saturated and ill-equipped to be embarking on the course. Some even said they would feel depressed and 'not good enough' and that this would have a negative effect on their future learning. This then led to members of the group speaking about their personal response to completing Form B.

One woman told us a story about her bus trip to the training venue earlier that morning. She spoke about what self-doubt and self-criticism had been trying to convince her of and the dominant discourses that were supporting self-doubts' claims: 'Everyone else will have more experience than you, you won't be able to handle the course, you shouldn't be doing this, your qualifications are not good enough, you won't be good enough, you don't have the right qualifications and background, it's going to be too hard, you won't cope with it, everyone will be more skilled than you, what have you got to offer?' She shared how completing Form B had helped her to reconnect with her own knowledges about her abilities and strengths. She said, 'I felt so much better. It helped me realise that I've got so much to contribute and that pieces of paper don't count for everything.'

This experience of reconnecting with alternative (preferred) stories of themselves as learners and people was common for many of the group members. Others talked about how the questions in Form B had made preferred stories of themselves as learners more available and had challenged some dominant cultural assumptions about knowledge that they were interested in thinking more about. 'I feel so relieved to know that people will be interested in me as a person and my uniqueness, that I won't be measured by what pieces of paper I've got ... that other parts of my life and experiences count as valuable.'

This sense of relief was shared by many people in the group. They spoke of how they felt that a burden had been lifted from them and that this was very helpful for them. They thought it would allow them more freedom to involve themselves in the course, to ask questions, to give their ideas. They spoke about how the questions had set a context of safety for them. I was really moved to hear these stories and rather surprised at myself that I had not thought about the exercise in this way.

Finally, I was interested to know from the group what they thought about doing the activity.

- *Was it useful and interesting and, if so, why?*
- *What did you like?*
- *What might you be interested in thinking more about?*
- *What will you take into your life from doing this?*

Many people spoke of how they enjoyed answering Form B questions and that the exercise had significantly assisted them to connect with stories of themselves as learners and people that they preferred. It seemed as though this outcome was most important for many of them. I was interested that no-one spoke about the technicalities or theory of the work that had been identified on the whiteboard.

My reflections

This led me to think a lot about the terms 'teaching' and 'learning'. Several years ago I trained as a teacher and spent many years in schools. Educational discourses encouraged me to assume that it is a teacher's responsibility to plan for all the possible educational outcomes of every activity. It encouraged assessing the success of any lesson according to whether or not the learning outcomes were achieved, placing little emphasis on the fact that very rich learning experiences could happen outside of these predetermined outcomes. It certainly did not encourage teachers to watch out for these unpredicted possibilities or regard them as possibly of utmost importance. It now seems an amazing idea to me that one person could predict all of the outcomes in a learning situation.

Since spending time with this group I've thought a lot about how teaching and my conversations with people who consult me have many similarities. It has had me reflecting upon how educational discourses invited me into assuming the position of expert in learning contexts - to narrowly define what people will and will not know after they have participated. I've wondered how I may have narrowed possibilities both for me and my 'students' by assuming and predicting outcomes. What possibilities could be missed if we predict outcomes and use them as a measurement of success and 'learning'?

In therapy I am more interested in joining with people in an exploration with many possibilities. Of course, I keep in mind some possibilities for what may be useful or helpful to them, and I attempt to bring my skills and experience to bear in a respectful, open and collaborative manner. I consult people about the process as it occurs and am guided by the interests and knowledges of the people consulting me. I attempt to be vigilant about accountability practices and am interested in knowing the effect of my conversations on peoples' lives. I never know at the beginning where the conversation will lead and often find so many rich and vivid outcomes that I would never have predicted. Why is a teaching context any different? I ask myself.

Notes

1. First published in the 1998 Vol.1 *Gecko*. Republished here with permission.

2. Alice can be contacted c/- Dulwich Centre Publications, Hutt St PO Box 7192, Adelaide 5000, South Australia, or on email: alicem3@ibm.net

3. The layout of these forms does not represent the spaces given to each question on the original forms.

4. The following discussion is my recollection of the comments from the group. Unfortunately, I rubbed off all the answers (not anticipating being asked to write about the exercise). I have consulted the group members subsequently to check their accuracy.

PART VII

Reflections
on
Practice

15

Curiosity didn't kill
the cat![1]

by

Louise Johnson[2]

The cat is alive and well. I can see him through the window, curled up in his
usual spot under the cedar tree. Such a creature of habit I have not known
before. He likes to eat the same foods at the same times and sleep in the same
places each day. His comings in and going outs are as predictable as the arrival
of the barley bugs. Even the daily being chased by the dog seems to be
ritualised. There is good reason for his cautious lifestyle. Curiosity, it would
seem, can be hazardous to cats. It is not, however, for humans.

This awareness about curiosity came, like a small shy bird, one lazy
Sunday morning. I was watching a film about the Dalai Lama, who happens to
be one of my most favourite people in all the world. I was captivated so it was
with some sense of annoyance that I realised my fourteen-month-old nephew
has tired of playing with the toys on the loungeroom floor and has now gone in
search of more distant horizons. I follow the trail of blocks to the bathroom to
discover that Michael has worked out how to open the cupboard in there. He
turns to me and flashes his 'don't you think I'm clever and much, much too cute
to growl at' smile. I agree on both counts and sit down on the floor next to him,

waiting to see what will happen next. A myriad of colour, shape, size, texture beams from the cupboard. Reaching in he selects a tin of powder and hands it to me. Making sure the lid is closed, I hand it back to him. Using the sense he most prefers, the tin is examined with his mouth. That doesn't hold any fascination for him so he hands the tin back to me. I open the lid and sprinkle some powder onto the back of his hand then hold it to my nose and sniff loudly. He laughs but doesn't get the idea of smelling it himself so I hold his hand to his nose. It wrinkles and crinkles and then he laughs as though with delight. Out comes his tongue and the hand is licked, sucked. Again, his nose wrinkles and crinkles. This time there's no delight.

This is how we came to be on the bathroom floor surrounded by the cupboard's contents, all of which have been carefully explored and examined, when Michael's dad arrives to collect him. Michael's dad has had a weekend in the city and has much to tell. I'm very interested in hearing about the tour through the Hanson Centre for cancer research. I hear how the guide his group had had was a young Ph.D student who'd recently discovered something new and useful about pre-cancerous cells. This discovery is considered to be a world breakthrough and has been met with much acclaim. I found myself thinking how amazing it was that anyone could discover anything new about cells, considering how many people, for so many years, have been looking at them through microscopes. In fact, it seems astounding to me that someone could still find something that has always been there but has not previously been recognised or known. Then it dawns on me that this is exactly what happens in Narrative Therapy - all sorts of 'amazing breakthroughs' are made when people recognise a skill or competency or belief or attitude that has long been with them and which, having been recognised, allows them to move into preferred terrains.

Only after Michael and his dad leave do I realise that someone else had joined us, been present all morning, and was, in fact, still with me. She was only small, which might explain why I hadn't noticed her until now - though not very adequately because, taking a good look, I can't imagine how I missed seeing her, with her bare feet, her wild, wild hair, and her deep, dark, sparkling black eyes. There's something mischievous, playful about her, completely compelling and endearing. I find myself enchanted and ask her to tell me about herself. She begins by telling me that she has been trying to catch my attention for ages now, but I've been too busy listening to Shame and Fear to take any notice of her. She tells me that her name is Curiosity and she asks me if I'd be interested in hearing about her work in Narrative Therapy practices. I tell her that I'd love to hear about this and wonder if she can begin immediately and tell me everything she knows - right now! Patiently, she explains that what she can impart to me has much more to do with a style, a way of being, than it does with any set techniques or standard questions that could be asked. I hear that, while there are maps to follow, the map can't be chartered beforehand, only worked out in collaboration with the person consulting me and that it is impossible to know where we are going, only to know where we are in the present, and perhaps some hoped-for directions; that the questions become part of a real exchange, of a moment-by-moment connectedness that has to do with a relatedness that is living, breathing, organic, dynamic, evolving. She tells me that the people consulting me and their lived experiences, preferences, interpretations, meanings, hopes, dreams, stories, stay at the centre of our conversation.

Curiosity tells me that it is my responsibility to create a space that feels safe and respectful, and that I can do this by continually checking with people about their experience of my questions and the shape of the conversation, asking about their preferences. She says that, seeing as though I mostly work with young people, it is good if I can include creativity and playfulness in this space as well. I ask her how I might possibly do this. She suggests inviting Imagination to join us and points to the types of questions that David Epston asks in his work with children, especially in his 'discovering discoveries' approach (Smith & Nylund 1997; Freeman, Epston & Lobovits 1997). 'Oh yes!' I say as I remember the way he offers some possibilities and then asks 'or what?', suggesting all sorts of domains, like magic or mental karate or conversations with puppies or inviting tigers to lunch - things that really invite the young person to access their own unique skills and knowledges.

Curiosity tells me that Narrative Therapists ask questions with the hope of 'generating experience', especially experience of preferred realities, *rather than to gather information* (Freeman & Combs 1996, p.113). Looking me in the eye, she goes on to say that, for several reasons, this is just so important in Narrative Therapy. She tells me that Power and Control (directors of the Dominant Culture Company in which I seem to have some shares) always presume that they have a right to know, a right to any information they choose.

A Narrative Therapist, she says, believes that they never, not ever, have a right to know anything about anyone else's life, only their own, and that they would always hope to be mindful of the relationship that exists between Knowledge and Power. I nod to show her I understand a little about this, as I recall the times when others have asked me questions because they've wanted information about me which I would rather not have given them. Curiosity tells me that she is always: *oriented towards people's strengths and competencies, and not towards their faults or deficits* (Monk, Winslade, Crocket & Epston 1997, p.88).

I am listening intently so Curiosity continues. She tells me that if I can adopt a 'not-knowing stance' (Smith & Nylund 1997, p.43) then I can concentrate on listening. As I listen I need to notice my thinking and question any assumptions I might be making, to check if I am accurately understanding what it is like to be this person and to make sure I am not filling in gaps with my own vivid imagination. I burst out laughing when I hear her say this. 'What's so funny?' Curiosity enquires. I tell her this reminds me of the time I was meeting with a nine-year-old boy who was telling me about the Bad Moods. He was saying it was like there was a fly buzzing around inside his chest. My mind immediately began to fill with an image of a pesky, annoying fly and I was thinking pesky flies sure are like bad moods. I can definitely see the correlation. By some miracle, I thought to ask him if this buzzing fly was a good thing or a bad thing. When he said it was a good thing I almost fell off my chair! When I asked him why it was a good thing he told me that the fly said things like, 'Buzz, buzz, calm down, go and sit on your own, count to ten ...' and all sorts of helpful things. Wow! What a lesson for me! I'd really run on ahead but not even in the right direction! Then the boy said to me, 'You know what else?' I said, 'No, what?' To my complete surprise he told me how he'd swallowed a fly once. I asked if this was the same fly that helps him. He replied that 'of course it was!'. I asked if the fly was still there inside of his chest and learned that it was, which seemed rather wonderful to both of us as it meant that the fly might more easily be called upon to help when he needed it to.

I then recalled other times when Assumption had clouded my vision - like the time a friend was talking with me about anxiety. We'd got to the stage where I'd been asking her questions about the influence she was able to have over the life of anxiety. When I asked her what she'd call the things she'd been describing to me, I was expecting her to say 'self-care' or something similar.

Instead she said 'Vanqua', and described this magnificent warrior maid who stands up for justice and fairness. For weeks after this conversation my friend took Vanqua to work with her, where together they stood up for fairness and challenged successfully the unjust practices that had given anxiety so much reign.

Despite having these valuable learning experiences, I know that Assumption is so sneaky and that I haven't yet wised up enough to its tricks, so I ask Curiosity if she will help me be on my guard against Assumption. She promises me that she will help me to think up questions that privilege the other person's descriptions, meanings and interpretations of experience so that I can learn from the person consulting me and learn especially about their alternative story.

Curiosity begins to wonder aloud if I've had enough of this conversation for today. I tell her, 'No way!', so she continues. She tells me that genuine interest and wonderment are like an antenna that enables the therapist to pick up and tune into glossed over or dismissed potential 'unique outcomes', and that as the therapist expresses curiosity about these things, it is like *life is breathed into these moments and collectively these previously isolated moments can form the building blocks of 'new' and 'alternative' stories* (Smith & Nylund 1997, p.36).

Breathing life into moments seems to me like breathing air into a balloon. Without the air a balloon is just a little insignificant thing, yet inflated it is a symbol of celebration and fun. Last week I had a conversation with a thirteen-year-old girl that was just like blowing up balloons. Her homegroup teacher had made an appointment for her to come and talk with the student counsellor and I. She walked into my office saying, 'I don't want to be here! I don't need to be here! I don't have a problem. Mrs X made me come.' We assured her that we would not want her to come or to stay against her will but, before she went, could we ask her a few questions? She reluctantly agreed. The student counsellor asked why she thought the teacher wanted her to meet with us. She said that it was because she'd had a really bad day that day but that was okay because now bad days were rare, whereas earlier in the year every day was bad. After seeking her permission for some more questions, we began to ask how this change had come about. We heard a story about fighting and about how this young woman had learned to decline invitations to join in, and we heard about the advice she'd been able to give herself especially in relation to when and when not to give her opinion about certain things. We heard how she has been able to reclaim ground in friendships that had been lost to her by making and valuing small steps. In the end she stayed for an hour. After she left, the student counsellor said to me that he didn't think this young woman always chose to act in the ways she'd described to us. I said that was why our conversation was so important, because it had breathed life into these other knowledges of ways of being that this person had that were right for her. Then I asked if he'd noticed all the balloons that had been floating on the ceiling before the young woman took them out with her. We felt happy and began to wonder what there was in our own lives that we could celebrate.

Remembering this day, I say, 'This work is fun, isn't it!' Curiosity nods her agreement and I know that her presence has a lot to do with what makes Narrative practices unique among therapies. Almost as though she could read my mind, Curiosity asks if I've heard that Hubble & O'Hanlon (Smith & Nylund 1997, p.22) say some therapists suffer from 'delusions of certainty and hardening of the categories'. We laugh long about this. I begin to think how boring it must be to have to be an expert, to have to assess, classify, evaluate, judge, and, worst of all, know all the right answers! I can see how Curiosity acts as a safeguard against the therapist privileging their own knowledge, skills, experience, beliefs, and would keep them from taking over the authorship of stories that belong to others.

I wonder what else Curiosity safeguards against. There's something very refreshing, invigorating, energising about being with her. I have some sense that she has another way of seeing, sort of naive or lateral. I think about how I've seen her at work with other therapists and realise that somehow she manages not to take for granted the taken-for-granted tenets of dominant culture. I wonder how she does this, so I ask her. She tells me that sometimes she teams up with Imagination or Childlikeness and that she really likes to team up with Persistence. 'Who?' I say, shocked. She says that she understands my surprise, but goes on to explain that if Persistence is going to be present, then it is essential that Curiosity and Respectfulness are also on the team. Without the other two, Persistence might team up with Interrogation, which is then destructive and disastrous. I can imagine this. I'm still puzzled why Persistence would be there at all. Persistence, Curiosity says, really helps to unpack those taken-for-granted assumptions and ideas that can be so subjugating of people's lives. Because they're taken-for-granted and so much a part of the dominant story, deconstructing them is not easy but, once people see how the problem-saturated story has been constructed, they begin to see how they might re-tell their story in a way that suits them, in a way that honours and acknowledges their own indigenous knowledges, skills, experience. Curiosity says that to *develop the alternative story 'smalling questions' often need to be asked and this requires patience and persistence* (Monk, Winslade, Crocket & Epston 1997, p.89).

What on earth are 'smalling questions', I ask. Smalling questions, she explains, are a way of finding little pieces that make up the jigsaw puzzle of the alternative story; questions that help to uncover a vague memory or a seemingly insignificant moment or an experience that doesn't fit with the problem-saturated story. Questions like: 'Are there small areas in your life where the problem has not yet been able to go?' or 'Are there any brief moments you can recall where the problem wasn't able to push you around?' A smalling question helps to open up space for discovery where one can explore those possibilities of which one is not yet aware (Monk, Winslade, Crocket & Epston 1997, p.89).

I sigh deeply. I can see that I need to allow Persistence some space in my work. I give up too easily. I get stuck. I can see that, like an archaeologist, I need Persistence to keep on shifting dirt until those fragments out of which the alternative story might be constructed, are uncovered.

This conversation with Curiosity has been wonderful for me. So much for me to think about, hope for. The sun has almost completed its daily journey, and outside the paddocks are glowing with a rosy hue.

Already the moon, a huge luminous orange ball, is showing her beautiful face low in the peachy pink sky. I wonder what tomorrow will bring and feel excited about returning to work. I'm hoping Curiosity will be there with me so that I can continue to consult with her. There's so much more she can teach me. I smile at her. All of a sudden the peace of dusk is pierced by a familiar, demanding sound. It's the cat at the door. Time for his tea. Curiosity and I look at each other and laugh. 'I must be going', she says, 'so that you can let the cat in'. I wonder what would really happen if Curiosity did chance to meet the cat, but figure it's better not to risk it - after all, everyone knows that Curiosity is hazardous to cats, don't they? I'm so glad it's not the case for humans.

Notes

1. First published in the 1999 Vol.1 *Gecko*. Republished here with permission.
2. Louise can be contacted c/- Dulwich Centre Publications, Hutt St PO Box 7192, Adelaide 5000, South Australia.

References

Epston, D. & White, M. 1992: *Experience, Contradiction, Narrative & Imagination.* Adelaide: Dulwich Centre Publications.

Freedman, J. & Combs, G. 1996: *Narrative Therapy: The social construction of preferred realities.* New York: Norton.

Freeman, J., Epston, D. & Lobovits, D. 1997: *Playful Approaches to Serious Problems.* New York: Norton.

Monk, G., Winslade, J., Crocket, K. & Epston, D. 1997: *Narrative Therapy in Practice: The archaeology of hope.* San Francisco: Jossey-Bass Inc.

Smith, C. & Nylund, D. 1997: *Narrative Therapies with Children & Adolescents.* New York: Guilford Press.

White, C. & Hales, J. (eds) 1997: *The Personal is The Professional.* Adelaide: Dulwich Centre Publications.

White, M. 1995: *Re-Authoring Lives: Interviews & essays.* Adelaide: Dulwich Centre Publications.

White, M. 1997: *Narratives of Therapists' Lives.* Adelaide: Dulwich Centre Publications.

White, M. & Epston, D. 1990: *Narrative Means to Therapeutic Ends.* New York: Norton.

Narrative Therapy and Community Work Conference

Adelaide 2000
February 16th-18th

We are excited to let you know that the second Dulwich Centre Publications' *Narrative Therapy and Community Work Conference* is to be held in Adelaide, South Australia, from 16th-18th February 2000. Seeing as there was such a good response to our inaugural conference, we're doing it again. The conference is to be surrounded by a week of events - ranging from a women's gathering, workshops, to our own mini-festival!

The Conference aims to gather together practitioners from a wide range of backgrounds and experiences who are involved in exciting and hopeful work informed by narrative ideas and practices. Many of the structures will be similar to those of our inaugural conference - we will try to create a number of different forums throughout the three days in which a variety of different sorts of conversations can take place. These will include: keynote addresses, two and a half hour practice-based seminars, one hour formal workshops, small group discussions under gum trees and umbrellas, evening workshops and sessions in a large marquee on the lawns. On the Thursday evening there will be a picnic dinner and concert.

For a full brochure about the conference, the workshops and extra events that we are organising, please contact:

Dulwich Centre Publications
Hutt St PO Box 7192
Adelaide 5000
phone (61-8) 8223 3966
fax: (61-8) 8232 4441
email: dulwich@senet.com.au
webpage: www.dulwichcentre.com.au